MW01014037

# THE RANCHO GORDO
# VEGETARIAN KITCHEN

# THE RANCHO GORDO VEGETARIAN KITCHEN

EVERYDAY COOKING with HEIRLOOM BEANS,
VEGETABLES, GREENS, and GRAINS

BY STEVE SANDO
AND JULIA NEWBERRY

RANCHO GORDO PRESS

DEDICATION:

This book is dedicated to the memory of Marcella Hazan. She wasn't a vegetarian but her respect for vegetables makes eating less meat a lot easier.

PHOTOGRAPHS by Steve Sando, except photos on page 9 (Nico Sando) and page 10 (Brian Newberry).

BOOK DESIGN by Meghan Hildebrand.

With thanks to Anita Crotty for copyediting and Ellen Sherron for indexing.

Lyrics for "Dirt Made My Lunch" reprinted by permission of the Banana Slug String Quartet (www.bananaslugstringband.com).

Copyright 2017 Rancho Gordo Press. All rights reserved. No part of this book may be reproduced in any form without written permission from the publisher.

ISBN: 978-0-692-94337-3

Printed in China.

10 9 8 7 6 5 4 3 2

Rancho Gordo Press
1924 Yajome St, Napa, CA 94559
www.ranchogordo.com

# CHAPTER 1: WHITE & LIGHT BEANS

# CHAPTER 2: MEDIUM-BODIED BEANS

# CHAPTER 3: DARK & HEARTY BEANS

# CHAPTER 4: NON-NATIVES & GRAINS

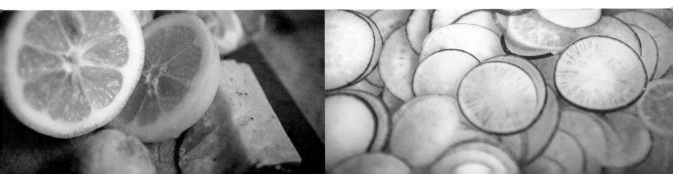

# LET'S MAKE GREAT FOOD

I've always felt that a huge part of the problem with vegetarian and vegan cooking is the focus on restrictions. "Don't eat this! Or that!" "Meat is evil!" It strikes me that showcasing delicious food made with fresh vegetables and grains is a much better way to encourage people to eliminate meat. Make the food so tempting that there really is no choice: This is what you should be eating. This is what you want to eat.

I'm an omnivore, but I find I'm eating less and less meat these days, especially as I become a better cook. Anyone can slap a steak on the grill, but it takes a bit of care to make beans into something creamy and indulgent. (Though it's not hard at all.) Raw carrots are fine, but tossing them with olive oil and roasting them makes you a magician. Add tahini sauce and you're a master magician. Combine all the vegetables in your crisper to build a feast, and you're approaching wizard status.

I've learned from a lot of amazing vegetable-inspired chefs in my life: Deborah Madison, Jeremy Fox, Annie Somerville, and legends like Marcella Hazan and Diana Kennedy, who we don't normally think of as vegetable-centric. None of these chefs is a strict vegetarian but each has spent a lifetime honoring vegetables. I remember a long time ago reading a Marcella Hazan recipe with very simple instructions and few ingredients. I decided to humor myself and follow her recipe to the letter. The results were spectacular.

My 16-year-old son is suddenly interested in eating well, in the interest of health and fitness. For Sunday supper, when my mother and another guest (or three) joins us, we cook whatever inspires us. But for the rest of the week, we eat mostly vegetarian meals. This plan is easy when we have a refrigerator full of roasted vegetables and cooked beans—and we almost always do.

If you've followed Rancho Gordo for a while, you'll notice that we rarely mention the health aspects of the beans and our other products. First of all, I'm uniquely unqualified to tell anyone the best way to eat. However, I also err on the side of caution. This week's "superfood" is next week's villain. My philosophy is that if you're eating real food, made with your own hands, you're probably doing fine. Aim toward whole grains and avoid sugar and you're better off than most.

In the end, I hate the idea of telling you what to do, and I'd rather encourage you instead. I hope you find lots of inspiring recipes in this book, whether or not you usually eat meat. Let's make great food.   —*Steve*

# THANK YOU, DIRT

My daughter learned a Banana Slug String Band song at preschool that I can't get out of my head. I will spare you the entire song, but the chorus goes:

*Dirt made my lunch,*
*Dirt made my lunch.*
*Thank you, Dirt,*
*Thanks a bunch.*
*For my salad, my sandwich,*
*My milk, and my munch.*
*'Cause, Dirt, you made my lunch!*

When I think about meal planning now, I focus on ingredients that come directly from dirt, preferably dirt from nearby. Where to start? Heirloom beans, of course. I've been working for Rancho Gordo long enough to know the specific patches of dirt that grow each of our bean varieties. I also know the characteristics of each type—the texture, the flavor, even the taste of the broth that develops as they cook.

I've found that if I use a pot of beans as a starting point, I can take endless directions based on what else I have available. Not one of those options needs to include meat. Although dried beans aren't really seasonal produce, they work as a base—and a complement—for whatever fresh vegetables have traveled from the dirt to my kitchen.

I'm not saying I don't buy premade foods, packaged snacks for my kids, or even meat. I do. But when I'm in the grocery store, the Dirt song echoes in my head, and I linger in the produce section. Did I miss anything? What about that broccoli rabe tucked in next to the broccoli heads? Or those little Persian cucumbers?

I want my family to celebrate the diversity of foods available to us. Rather than hiding pureed spinach in pasta sauce, or cooking the same steamed green beans every night because I'm certain my kids will eat them, I'd like every meal to be a new reason to thank the dirt for what it provides. Of course, that's easier said than done, but it's a goal.

I remember the first time Steve told me he was frustrated with the constant pressure to churn out recipe after recipe. His mission, I realized, was encouraging people to enjoy the distinct flavors of heirloom beans before combining them with 15 other ingredients. This actually made perfect sense to me, even though I had been a cookbook editor before joining the Rancho Gordo team. But, still, the big question we hear from customers is: "Do you have a recipe for this bean?" So here we are, wanting to help.

We want this cookbook to be your companion for everyday meals. We've organized the recipes by bean variety, hoping that you might already have a batch of cooked beans at the ready, looking for ways to be useful. Steve and I tend toward different cooking styles, but we both agree that a focus on simplicity and quality is the key to keeping heirloom beans, seasonal vegetables, and grains at the center of your plate. *—Julia*

# ABOUT THIS BOOK

On Mondays, Julia and I often compare notes about the food we made
over the weekend. Sometimes one of
us hosted an elaborate dinner party.
Sometimes, it's been a full weekend
of shoving something sort-of-healthy
into a hungry kid's mouth. But food is
always there.

Even when I am trying to eat a little
less indulgently, I avoid the terms
"cleanse" and "clean eating," and never
think of my food as a puritan practice.
I love vegetables and farmers markets,
and my favorite place in a good grocery
store is the produce section. I also
know that more and more of our customers are looking for vegetarian ideas
and recipes. With all of those forces
coming together, this book was born.

Often, I'll post a photo on Instagram
with a description like "Beans and
leftover chard, tossed with some good
olive oil." Inevitably one or two people
will comment: "Recipe, please!" That
*was* the recipe.

Most of what I eat is simple food like
this, and I don't want to insult your
intelligence with inane filler, so we've
added what I call *Quick Ideas* among
the recipes in this book.

At first, we were torn over how to orga-
nize this book. Categorizing recipes by
course seemed arbitrary; one person's
salad is another's main course. Since
beans are the stars of our show, we
decided to split the book by type: white
and light beans, medium-bodied beans,
dark beans, and non-natives and grains.
Many beans are interchangeable within
these categories, but we've made some
suggestions. If you make a substitution,
the texture and flavor of the bean you
choose may be different than the specific bean in the recipe, but it will still
be delicious.   —*Steve*

Pre-Cabernet tasting
American Heritage tasting

olives
radishes
ceviche
salad
} Toppers

Charro Beans — yogurt
                  walnut

Taco Buffet.
Poached Chicken
Mexican Sausage
Chipotle Salsa
Tomatillo Salsa
roasted tomatillo
watermelon / salad

crema fresca 10

# WHITE & LIGHT BEANS

### ALUBIA BLANCA

A small, versatile Spanish-style white bean. It has a creamy texture and thin skin but still manages to hold its shape.

### AYOCOTE BLANCO

A super-rich midsize white bean. Ayocote Blanco hold their shape through long cooking but manage to stay creamy. A versatile runner bean.

### CASSOULET (TARBAIS)

West Coast-grown from classic French Tarbais seed stock. The most famous bean for a traditional cassoulet but versatile enough to become an everyday favorite.

### FLAGEOLET

A super mild European-style classic heirloom bean, known for its pairing with lamb but excellent as a pot bean and with roasted tomatoes.

### LARGE WHITE LIMA

Lima beans have a creamy texture and savory flavor and they taste more like fresh vegetables than other beans. New-crop Large White Lima beans are quick-cooking and delicious and worthy of your attention, especially if you grew up eating those nasty frozen Lima beans.

### MARCELLA (CANNELLINI)

From heirloom Italian seed, this thin-skinned cannellini is named after Italian cooking hero Marcella Hazan, who encouraged our growing it. A delicate tribute to a mighty force of nature.

### ROYAL CORONA

An enormous, thick-skinned runner bean with a surprisingly creamy interior. One of our all-time best sellers, it's a versatile giant that works in all kinds of cuisines. A true pantry staple.

### WHITE TEPARY

A small, hearty, and dense bean that's drought-tolerant and indigenous to the American southwest. White Tepary beans are slightly sweeter than Brown Tepary beans.

# MEDIUM-BODIED BEANS

### CRANBERRY

Versatile and velvety, this thin-skinned Borlotti bean produces a rich, indulgent bean broth, making it perfect for classic Italian dishes as well as simple pot beans.

### MAYOCOBA

Creamy and versatile, Mayocoba has a pale yellow hue and super soft texture. This mild-flavored bean soaks up all the flavors of the cooking pot.

### PINTO

The classic bean. Soft, creamy, and versatile, our Pintos cook quickly and create converts to new crop, heirloom beans.

### SANTA MARIA PINQUITO

The small, dense orbs produce a beefy bean broth. An essential ingredient in California cuisine, they are the heart of a tri-tip barbecue and yet they're perfectly at home in meatless meals.

### YELLOW EYE

Rich, creamy, and mild, this best-seller is delicious without fuss. Essential for New England baked beans but versatile enough for almost any cuisine.

### YELLOW INDIAN WOMAN

Small, dense yet velvety bean that holds its shape and provides a rich bean broth. Easily one of the staff's favorite beans.

# DARK & HEARTY BEANS

## AYOCOTE MORADO

This thick-skinned purple bean (produced in Mexico) is pretty and very large. It's starchy but goes from dense to creamy with continued cooking.

## AYOCOTE NEGRO

Nearly identical to Ayocote Morados in size, texture, and flavor, Ayocote Negros are jet black.

## BROWN TEPARY

A small, hearty and dense bean that's drought-tolerant and indigenous to the American southwest.

## CHRISTMAS LIMA

A rich chestnut texture and an almost nutty flavor make this the most unusual Lima bean. A true revelation for those who believe they don't like Lima beans.

## DOMINGO ROJO

A classic red bean, essential to dishes like New Orleans Red Beans & Rice, and equally important to many Caribbean cuisines. Domingo Rojo holds its shape when cooked, and the thick bean broth coats every rice grain or noodle with a luxurious sauce.

## EYE OF THE GOAT

Our famous bean with the velvety texture and deep bean broth. A favorite classic pot bean that needs little adornment.

## GOOD MOTHER STALLARD

Deep rich flavor, velvety texture and an addicting bean broth make Good Mother Stallard almost everyone's favorite bean.

## LILA

Pretty purple beans also known as "Frijol Apetito." Nice, isn't it? When cooked, it's juicy and velvety and everything you might want in a bean.

## MIDNIGHT BLACK

A classic, versatile, essential black turtle bean. It holds its shape through lots of cooking yet retains its famous creamy interior. The bean broth can be used as a base for all kinds of soups.

## MORO

Beautiful markings and a dense, rich flavor make this super-rare bean a favorite. Almost a marriage between a black bean and a pinto but unique in its own right.

## REBOSERO

An heirloom passed down for generations in rural Hidalgo, Mexico, this small, compact bean produces a rich, flavorful broth.

## RIO ZAPE

The classic heirloom bean that inspired the birth of Rancho Gordo. Suggestions of chocolate and coffee make this pinto-family rarity one of our favorite and most requested beans.

### SAN FRANCISCANO

Pinto flavor with a denser texture, these heirlooms from Mexico produce a dark, rich bean broth.

### SANGRE DE TORO

From central Mexico, Sangre de Toro manages to be dense without being starchy. Its famous bean broth makes it a natural for all kinds of rice-and-bean dishes.

### SCARLET RUNNER

Big, beefy runner bean with gorgeous markings. Cooks from starchy to creamy and is a constant chef's favorite.

### VAQUERO

A classic chili bean that holds its shape through long, slow, cooking and exudes a generous, dark, rich broth.

# NON-NATIVES & GRAINS

## GARBANZO BEANS

A slightly nutty-flavored classic bean, essential for Middle Eastern, Mexican, and European cooking. Garbanzos aren't a true "new world" bean, but we love them so much and the imported crops tend to be so old and dusty that we make this one of our California crops. New-crop harvest ensures quicker cooking and fresher flavor.

## BLACK EYED PEAS

All good Southerners and their friends know the secret to a prosperous New Year (and beyond) is to eat old-fashioned Black Eyed peas on New Year's Day. Cooking new-crop peas from Rancho Gordo ensures that your years will be tastier, as well.

## POSOLE (PREPARED HOMINY)

The essential nixtamalized grain, prepared in small batches, for hominy stews. After a gentle simmer, dried hominy opens up like a delicious flower and is ready to use in soups, stews and the classic southwestern and Mexican dish, Pozole (or Posole). The corn is prepared by removing the skins after soaking them in the mineral lime (cal), which changes the flavor (for the better) and releases the niacin, making this slightly processed grain healthier than simple dried corn or cornmeal.

## QUINOA

The versatile "Mother Grain" from the Andes. Full of protein, full of flavor, naturally gluten-free and adaptable to almost any cuisine, quinoa has taken over as the grain of choice for a lot of us. It's quick cooking and works as a replacement for rice, couscous or pasta. Don't forget to add it to soups and stews!

## WILD RICE

Wild rice is not a true rice but an aquatic seed. One of the New World's native grains, wild rice has too long been stuck on the holiday table or teamed with salmon and little else. Don't let odd marketing fool you: wild rice is a great everyday grain. It has a great chewy texture and distinct nutty flavor.

# COOKING A POT OF BEANS
# IN THE RANCHO GORDO MANNER

There's no right way to cook beans, and there's only one actual rule: Simmer the beans in a pot until they're soft.

Soaking can speed up the process. Adding broth, seasonings, or vegetables will make the beans more flavorful. It's really that simple. There are different methods and small changes you might make, but basically, this is it.

Normally on a bean-cooking day (which, frankly, is every day at Rancho Gordo), I put the beans to soak in the morning, after rinsing them in lots of cool water and checking for small debris. I cover the beans with water by about an inch or so. If you haven't soaked your beans, don't fret. Go ahead and cook them unsoaked, knowing it will take a bit longer.

Heirloom and heritage bean varieties don't need a lot of fussing so long as they are used within two years of harvest. I usually start with a classic mirepoix—a mix of onion, celery, and carrot, all diced fine—sautéed in some kind of fat, often olive oil. A crushed garlic clove doesn't hurt.

Add the beans and their soaking water to a large pot. You probably were taught to change the water and rinse the beans. But current nutritional wisdom holds that vitamins and flavor leech out of the beans into the soaking water, which you end up throwing down the drain. There's conflicting scientific evidence as to whether or not changing the water cuts down on the digestive gas that eating beans can produce. But it's your choice: If you want to get rid of the soaking water, do it; if it seems unnecessary, don't bother.

If you've soaked the beans, they will have expanded, so make sure they are still covered by a couple inches of water in the pot. Add the sautéed vegetables to the beans and give everything a good stir. Raise heat to medium-high and bring the liquid to a hard boil. Keep the beans boiling for 10–15 minutes. After so many years of paying attention to beans, I think this is the moment that really matters: You have to give the beans a good, hard boil to let them know you're the boss, then reduce them to a gentle simmer before covering. I like to see how low I can adjust the flame and still get the occasional simmering bubble. Open and close the lid, or keep it ajar, to help control heat and allow some evaporation. The bean broth will taste its best if it has had a chance to breathe and reduce a little.

The aroma will fill the room when the beans are almost ready. You'll no longer smell the vegetables you've cooked, but the beans themselves. At this point, go ahead and salt them. Go easy on the salt at first, and taste the beans after a bit more cooking; it takes a while for them to absorb the salt. If you want to add tomatoes, or acids like lime juice or vinegar, wait until the beans are cooked completely.

If the bean water starts getting low, always add hot water. Many cooks believe that cold water added to simmering beans will harden them. We're not convinced, but it *will* make the cooking take longer, because you'll need to bring the beans back to a simmer. We don't recommend using hot tap water, though. It's better to heat cool tap water in a kettle or saucepan first.

After patiently waiting, simmering, and tasting for tenderness, you're done! Once you've mastered this method, go ahead and try a few different techniques, if you like. Your bean-loving friends will swear by this or that method. Try them, if you want, keeping in mind there are few absolutes. It's hard work to mess up a pot of beans, as long as you're paying attention.

### WHAT'S NEXT?

We encourage you to taste a simple bowl of beans before gussying them up or adding them to a recipe. If you want to add a topping, how about a drizzle of your best olive oil, a dusting of Parmesan cheese or Rancho Gordo Stardust Dipping Powder, or a sprinkle of chopped fresh herbs?

### OTHER TOPPING IDEAS FOR A SIMPLE BOWL OF BEANS:

Your favorite salsa (see page 150 and 151 for recipes)

Roasted Poblano Chile Rajas (page 148)

Requesón (page 151)

Fried tortilla strips (page 107)

Tzatziki (page 138)

Italian-Style Salsa Verde (page 150)

# COOKING BEANS IN A SLOW COOKER

Every day at Rancho Gordo, our retail staff cooks a batch of our heirloom beans in the Crock Pot for customer samples. This is how they do it.

*1 pound Rancho Gordo beans*

*2 garlic cloves, finely chopped*

*½ of a small onion (preferably white), finely chopped*

*1 tablespoon extra-virgin olive oil*

*1 tablespoon dried Mexican oregano, preferably Rancho Gordo Oregano Indio*

*1 tablespoon kosher salt*

Check beans for small debris and rinse in cool water. Depending on how much time you have, you can soak the beans or cook them right away. Soaking the beans will reduce the cooking time by 1–2 hours, depending on the bean variety. If you choose to soak, cover the beans with 2 inches of water and soak for 4–6 hours.

Place the beans in the slow cooker and cover with about 2 inches of water. Add the garlic, onion, and olive oil. Add the oregano, crushing it with your hand to release the flavor.

Put the lid on the slow cooker and cook the beans on high for 3–4 hours for soaked beans (or 4–5 hours for unsoaked beans). Check the beans occasionally for doneness to avoid over-cooking. Once the beans are nearly done, add the salt, cover, and cook until beans are soft.

# COOKING BEANS IN A PRESSURE COOKER

It's best to consult the manufacturer's instructions for your pressure cooker's preferred method. If your manual's lost in the junk drawer, this is the basic idea, although you may need to experiment with timing and ratios in order to discover what works best.

Place cleaned beans in the pressure cooker and cover with three to four parts water. Cook under pressure for 20 minutes and release. Simmer, with the lid off, for another 20 minutes.

# BEANS AND GREENS

Pair any leftover heirloom beans with sautéed greens for a quick and delicious meal.

My standard technique includes washing the greens, then adding them—still wet—to a skillet full of simmering onions, garlic, chiles, and olive oil. Salt and stir, and soon enough you have a bowl full of good greens. Add a couple of cups of cooked heirloom beans and you have a meal.

For this type of dish, sturdy greens—like beet greens, broccoli rabe, chard, collards, dandelion, escarole, kale, mustard greens, nettles, purslane, or spinach—work best.     *—Steve*


*2 tablespoons extra-virgin olive oil*

*1 small white or yellow onion, minced*

*2 garlic cloves, minced*

*½ of a serrano chile, minced*

*About 4 cups chopped greens, washed and still wet*

*About 2 cups cooked Rancho Gordo beans in their broth,
cooked as directed on page 22*

*Salt*


*Serves 2–4*


In a large skillet, warm the oil over medium heat. Add the onion; cook until soft, about 5 minutes. Add the garlic and chile; sauté until fragrant, about 2 minutes more. Add the wet greens and toss, stirring until wilted. (The timing will depend on the type of green you are using.)

Add the beans and their cooking liquid; stir gently until combined. Let simmer until some of the cooking liquid evaporates and the beans are warm. Add salt to taste.


## A NOTE ON PURSLANE:

I've been a fan of purslane for a long time. I first encountered purslane in the books of Diana Kennedy. In Spanish, it's known as *verdolagas* and often teamed with pork and tomatillos for a tangy stew that I love. I found it in my garden when I took up tomato growing and was pleased that the soft, succulent weed came up so easily by the root. You can add it raw to a salad, but I think it's best sautéed and used in simple soups or dishes like this.

# A PLEA FOR HEIRLOOM BEANS

When I first started Rancho Gordo, a dear old pal from my days as a dandy in San Francisco warned me that it probably wasn't the best idea to focus on heirloom beans. I ignored him. I think he was amused by my modest success as the years went by. At one point, he wrote and told me how much he loved one of our beans. He confessed it was the first time he'd actually cooked any heirlooms. He was shocked at the differences between our beans and plain old commodity beans. If this is what a very good friend—someone who listened to my passion for heirloom beans—experienced, I can only imagine what the average Joe thinks. A recipe from this book might look nice, but if you use red kidney beans from a dubious source, I don't think you'll get much out of this book.

Using the best ingredients available is always the goal, but for vegetarian cooking, it's essential. Without meat, flavors are more gentle and subtle. Why try and cut corners with your protein? You really do deserve better.

Heirlooms tend to yield smaller crops and are more difficult to grow, so the cost is higher than with supermarket beans. But, per serving, heirloom beans are still an excellent value. (If you're reading this book, I suspect you already know this.)   —*Steve*

*Chapter 1*

# WHITE & LIGHT BEANS

Light beans tend to be creamy and mild. European cuisines seem to favor them, but not exclusively. Because of their mildness, they are more versatile, and for many, they can be a great gateway to the world of beans.

I remember eating heirloom white runner beans for the first time. They were amazingly smooth and delicious, the opposite of how I perceived ordinary white navy beans. We have about five kinds of white beans available at any given time and even though they're all white, they have enough variation between texture, skin thickness, size, and taste that it's hard to imagine giving up any one of them.

*As a young fellow, I loved a rather nasty pinto bean dip that came in a can. I could eat it cold…and I often did. This recipe is a step up from that guilty pleasure, and it's delightfully easy. Rules are meant to be broken, so if you want to change the type of oil, add some peppers, or use a white onion, it's all up to you. This is one of those dishes that come to mind when people tell me they can't eat a pound of beans in a week. For that last cup, this is the answer.* —Steve

# HEIRLOOM WHITE BEAN DIP

*1 cup cooked Rancho Gordo Marcella, Ayocote Blanco, Cassoulet, or Alubia Blanca beans in their broth, cooked as directed on page 22*

*½ of a yellow onion, sliced very thin*

*1 tablespoon extra-virgin olive oil*

*1 teaspoon dried Mexican oregano, preferably Rancho Gordo Mexican Oregano or Oregano Indio*

*Kosher salt*

*Extra-virgin olive oil*

*Flat-leaf parsley, minced*

In a skillet, warm the olive oil over medium-low heat. Add the onions and cook until soft, about 15 minutes. Add the beans, their liquid, and the oregano. Stir to combine; remove from heat.

Puree the mixture with an immersion blender until smooth (or let cool slightly and process in a blender or food processor). Taste and adjust seasonings; add salt to taste.

Pour onto a platter. On the top of the dip, make a small "S" with your finger; drizzle with olive oil and sprinkle with parsley.

This recipe is best served at room temperature with crudites, crackers, or chips for dipping.

*Serves 4*

**MEXICAN OREGANO** is similar to European oregano but less sweet and with a slight citrus twist. There are many plants known as "oregano" in Mexico, but the variety that we sell as Rancho Gordo Mexican Oregano (*Lippia graveolens*) is the most common. Our Oregano Indio (*Poliomintha longiflora A. Gray*) is less citrusy than the standard Mexican oregano and there's an indescribable earthiness that makes it infectious.

# ALUBIA BLANCA BEAN SALAD WITH PINEAPPLE VINAIGRETTE

For the vinaigrette:

*1 garlic clove, minced*

*1 teaspoon salt*

*1 teaspoon Dijon mustard*

*1 teaspoon dried Mexican oregano, preferably Rancho Gordo Oregano Indio*

*2 tablespoons Rancho Gordo Pineapple Vinegar*

*½ cup extra-virgin olive oil*


*1 carrot, peeled*

*1½ cups cooked Rancho Gordo Alubia Blanca beans, cooked as directed on page 22, then drained*

*1 roasted red pepper, cut into ½-inch squares*

*3 radishes, thinly sliced*

*1 celery stalk, chopped*

*Salt and freshly ground pepper*

In a salad bowl, make a paste with the garlic and salt. Add the mustard, oregano, and pineapple vinegar; mix well. Slowly whisk in the olive oil.

Shave the carrot into razor-thin slices using a mandoline or vegetable peeler. Add the beans, roasted red pepper, radishes, celery, and carrot slices to the vinaigrette; toss together gently. Season with salt and pepper. Serve slightly chilled or at room temperature.

*Serves 2–4*

**THE BEST VINEGARS** are made from fermented fruit, like Rancho Gordo Pineapple Vinegar and Banana Vinegar. Make sure any vinegar you purchase is actually fermented, and not just apple cider vinegar with flavoring added.

*Even though they're soft and creamy, Alubia Blanca beans still hold their shape when cooked, which makes them one of the best salad beans. For me, the cream of the beans and the crunch of the celery and radish make for a great salad.* —*Steve*

*Panzanella is a Tuscan tomato-and-bread salad usually served in the summer. Once the temperature drops, a local favorite called Foodshed—a takeaway here in Napa that caters all of our important meetings and lunches—pairs the crunch of toasted bread with bright, slightly spicy olive oil, creamy beans, and ribbons of kale ... no tomatoes! It's a satisfying dish in the fall and winter when you're craving something hearty. The added bonus is that you can use up stale bread.    —Steve*

# WHITE BEAN AND KALE PANZANELLA

3–4 thick slices of crusty Italian bread

3–4 tablespoons extra-virgin olive oil or olio nuovo, plus more for tossing

Salt

¼ of a red onion, thinly sliced

¼ cup red wine vinegar

½ of a large bunch of Tuscan kale, leaves stripped from the stems and cut into 1-inch pieces

2 cups cooked Rancho Gordo white beans (such as Cassoulet, Royal Corona, Alubia Blanca, or Marcella) cooked as directed on page 22, then drained

Preheat the oven to 300°F. Remove the crust, if you like, then cut the bread into 1-inch cubes and toss with olive oil and salt. Scatter the seasoned bread cubes on a baking sheet, and toast them in the oven until golden, about 10 minutes.

In a small bowl, toss the onion with the vinegar; set aside for 15 minutes.

Meanwhile, in a large saucepan, cook the kale in boiling salted water over high heat until slightly soft, about 2 minutes; drain. When the kale has cooled, squeeze out most of the water.

Remove the onion from the vinegar. Gently toss the marinated onions with the beans and 3 tablespoons olive oil. Add the kale and adjust the seasoning; add more olive oil, vinegar from the onion marinade, and salt to taste. Fold in the toasted bread; serve immediately.

*Serves 4*

**ITALIAN BREAD SALADS** are traditionally made with white bread, but if there are no Italians around, try using whole-grain sourdough bread.

# ROASTED CARROT, HEIRLOOM BEAN, AND FARRO SALAD

*1 cup pearled farro or Rancho Gordo Emmer (farro medio)*

*5 tablespoons extra-virgin olive oil (divided use), plus more for drizzling*

*1 teaspoon dried Mexican oregano, preferably Rancho Gordo Oregano Indio*

*2 pounds slender carrots, scrubbed and halved lengthwise*

*6–10 garlic cloves, peeled and smashed*

*10 sprigs fresh thyme*

*¼ cup chopped flat-leaf parsley*

*1 red bell pepper, diced (optional)*

*1½–2 cups cooked Rancho Gordo Royal Corona, Ayocote Blanco or Cassoulet beans, cooked as directed on page 22, then drained*

*Salt and freshly ground pepper*

In a large saucepan, cover the farro with plenty of salted water. Bring to a boil, then reduce heat to low. Simmer the farro until the grains are al dente, 20–25 minutes for pearled farro and about 1 hour for Emmer (*farro medio*). Drain the farro and return to the pan. While the farro is still warm, toss it with 2 tablespoons olive oil and 1 teaspoon oregano; set aside.

Preheat the oven to 500°F.

In a large bowl, toss the carrots and garlic with about a teaspoon of salt, 3 tablespoons of olive oil, and the thyme sprigs. Arrange the seasoned carrots on a sheet pan in a single layer. If you have a gas oven, place the sheet pan directly on the floor of the oven. For an electric oven, use the bottom rack, preferably with a pizza stone. Cook for 6 minutes. Rotate and shake the pan; cook until the carrots cut easily with a fork, another 6–8 minutes. Remove from the oven; cool.

Discard the thyme. Toss the carrots, garlic, parsley, and red pepper (if using) with the farro. Very gently fold in the beans. Check seasoning; add salt, if desired. Arrange the salad on a serving platter and drizzle with a little more olive oil. Top generously with freshly ground pepper.

*Serves 6–8*

**FARRO** comes in many forms. Pearled farro is the quickest cooking. Rancho Gordo carries Emmer, also known in Italy as *farro medio*. It takes longer to cook, but I think the texture and the nutty flavor make up for it.

*One of my favorite recent books has been Nancy Silverton's* Mozza at Home. *I would describe my style of cooking as "rustic casual" and the book describes itself as "relaxed, family-style entertaining." A perfect match! Nancy's recipe for Roasted Carrots and Wheat Berry Salad with Dill is my jumping-off point for this recipe. I subbed in farro for wheat berries and Mexican oregano for dill, and I added some cooked Royal Corona beans, making the dish substantial enough for a main course.* —Steve

*If someone told me 10 years ago that I was going to write a recipe for a bean and brussels sprouts salad, I probably would have laughed. But now this salad is, to me, perfection: light, lemony, salty, and satisfying. Salting the sprouts tenderizes them and, of course, adds plenty of saltiness to the dish, but you can omit this step if you wish.* —*Julia*

# FLAGEOLET WITH SHAVED BRUSSELS SPROUTS AND LEMON

*1½ pounds brussels sprouts, very thinly sliced with a mandoline (about 4 cups sliced)*

*2 teaspoons kosher salt (optional; see note)*

*2 cups cooked Rancho Gordo Flageolet beans, cooked as directed on page 22, then drained*

*Zest of 2 lemons*

*Juice of 1 lemon*

*½ cup freshly grated pecorino romano cheese*

*A handful of roughly chopped toasted walnuts (preferably black walnuts)*

*Freshly ground pepper*

In a bowl, toss the shredded sprouts with the salt, if using. Mix well, kneading the sprouts with your hands to soften. Transfer to the refrigerator and let sit for at least 15 minutes and up to 4 hours. Remove the sprouts from the refrigerator. Using your hands, squeeze the sprouts to remove excess liquid.

Transfer sprouts to a serving bowl. Add the beans, lemon zest, juice, and cheese; stir well. Taste and adjust the seasonings. Top with walnuts and black pepper to taste.

*Serves 4–6 as a side dish*

**MANDOLINE** accidents happen, even when you're being careful. Steve and I both love our inexpensive Japanese models, but we recommend using the guard to protect your fingers.

# LUPE'S WHITE BEAN, CELERY, AND RADISH SALAD

½ of a red onion, thinly sliced

1 celery stalk, cut in half lengthwise, then cut into ¼-inch slices

⅓ cup chopped flat-leaf parsley

1 cucumber, thinly sliced

1 bunch of radishes, cleaned and trimmed, then thinly sliced

2½ cups cooked Rancho Gordo Royal Corona, Ayocote Blanco, or Cassoulet beans, cooked as directed on page 22, then drained

3 tablespoons extra-virgin olive oil

2 teaspoons Rancho Gordo Pineapple Vinegar

Salt and freshly ground pepper

Add all the ingredients to a large salad bowl and gently toss. Taste and adjust the seasonings. Serve at room temperature.

*Serves 4*

**A VEGETABLE PEELER** is a good tool for thinly slicing vegetables if you don't own a mandoline. I used a vegetable peeler to cut the radishes paper-thin, and I still have all my fingers intact. It's also a nice way to slice carrots. After you've gotten rid of the skins, keep peeling. The thin slices are great in salads.

*We used to host a bean tour with our Xoxoc partners in Mexico. They have a beautiful hacienda and Lupe, one of the matriarchs of the family, wowed everyone with her cooking. One night, Lupe was planning the meals and decided to make a salad with white beans, inspired by one of the recipes in my first book. A white bean salad is definitely not traditional Mexican fare, but everyone loved it, especially Lupe!*

*Lupe made her version with Ayocote Blanco beans, but you can use your favorite white variety. I prefer Royal Coronas because they are so ridiculously big.*     —Steve

*After spending so much time in San Francisco, I came to view fennel as a weed. My eyes rolled when others told me what a great vegetable it was. Years later, inspired by the* Moro *cookbooks by Sam and Sam Clark, I gave this soup a try. I've been a fennel fan ever since.* —Steve

# FENNEL, POTATO, AND WHITE BEAN SOUP

*½ pound Rancho Gordo Royal Corona or Cassoulet beans, picked over and rinsed (see page 22)*

*4 tablespoons extra-virgin olive oil, plus extra for drizzling*

*4 fennel bulbs, outside layer removed, halved, and finely chopped (fronds chopped and reserved for garnish)*

*2 garlic cloves, peeled and thinly sliced*

*3 medium waxy potatoes (about 1 pound total), peeled and diced*

*4–6 cups bean cooking liquid and/or water*

*A medium pinch of saffron (30–40 threads), soaked in 2 tablespoons boiling water*

*Salt and freshly ground pepper*

Cook the Royal Corona beans in the usual manner, as described on page 22. When finished, strain the beans and reserve the broth. (If you're using beans you've already cooked, you'll want about 2 cups of cooked beans.)

In a large frying pan, heat the oil over medium-high heat; add the fennel and a pinch of salt. Cook gently, stirring occasionally, for about 20 minutes. The fennel will start to caramelize and soften. If it begins to brown or burn, reduce the heat. Add the garlic and potatoes; continue cooking for another 5 minutes.

Add the bean broth (or water) and the saffron and its soaking water. Continue cooking until the potatoes are soft, about 10–12 minutes. Gently fold in the beans and cook another few minutes until the beans are warmed through. Stir in the fennel fronds.

Ladle into bowls and top each serving with a few additional fennel fronds and a drizzling of extra virgin olive oil.

*Serves 4*

**FENNEL** is perhaps more famous raw, but I love how it caramelizes when cooked. It's an essential part of my kitchen now.

*A soup course means the evening is bound to be full of good things. It means your host likes you enough to dirty a round of soup bowls. It may also mean you have a clever host who has found a way to use up odds and ends, and present them in a new way. I'm on board no matter what the story. This soup is velvety and mild. The salsa has little or no heat, but it's loaded with flavor. It's a nice accent to the beans and potatoes. The cream is a sign that this is a special occasion. Like many good dishes, this was born of leftovers. Some beans, some potatoes, and some salsa. Voilà! A soup course.* —Steve

# ALUBIA BLANCA AND POTATO SOUP WITH CASCABEL CHILE SALSA

*1 cup cooked Rancho Gordo Alubia Blanca, Royal Corona, or Ayocote Blanco beans, cooked as directed on page 22, then drained*

*2½ cups cooked potatoes (about 3 medium potatoes), cubed*

*2 cups liquid (leftover bean broth, potato cooking water, or a combination)*

*3 tablespoons Cascabel Chile Salsa (page 150)*

*2 tablespoons crema mexicana or sour cream*

*1 teaspoon dried Mexican oregano, preferably Rancho Gordo Oregano Indio*

*Salt*

In a large saucepan, combine the beans, potatoes, and cooking liquid. Puree the mixture with an immersion blender until smooth (or process in batches in a blender or food processor). Heat the puree over medium-low heat; simmer gently until the soup is thoroughly hot, about 10 minutes.

Remove from heat; add the salsa, crema, and oregano. Check seasonings and add salt to taste. Serve immediately. Garnish with more oregano, if you like.

*Serves 4–6 as a starter*

*Once you make a batch of Romesco Sauce, you will want to put it on everything: beans, salads, bread, grilled vegetables, grilled cheese sandwiches, pasta. You will also want to take a vacation to Spain. Start in Barcelona and make your way down the coast to Tarragona, where this sauce originated. This dish is easy enough for a weeknight but could also be elevated to dinner party status. Harness your inner chef and play around with the plating—smear some bright orange sauce on the bottom of the plate, top with the beans and then the potatoes, and finish with green, fragrant parsley.*     —*Julia*

# ALUBIA BLANCA BEANS WITH ROMESCO SAUCE AND CRISPY POTATOES

*1 pound small red- or white-skinned potatoes, halved*

*Olive oil*

*Salt and pepper*

*3 cups cooked Rancho Gordo white beans, such as Alubia Blanca, Cassoulet, or Royal Corona, cooked as directed on page 22, then drained*

*Romesco Sauce (page 149)*

*Chopped flat-leaf parsley for garnish*

Preheat oven to 400°F.

Place the potatoes in a bowl and toss with a generous amount of olive oil, salt, and pepper. Transfer to a baking dish large enough to spread them out in one layer. Place in the oven. Bake until the potatoes are golden and crisp on the outside and soft in the middle, about 45 minutes, flipping the potatoes halfway through cooking.

Meanwhile, in a small saucepan, warm the beans over low heat.

Smear a generous amount of Romesco Sauce on each plate, then top with the beans and potatoes. Garnish with parsley.

*Serves 4*

*Like so many people, I'm obsessed with fermenting. One of the best things to ferment is cabbage, which becomes sauerkraut over time. If you make your own sauerkraut, you may have an abundance, like I did. That bounty led to this dish and even though most sauerkraut recipes seem to pair kraut with fatty meats, my soup came out vegan. I served this to guests who were adamantly against sauerkraut and they loved it. You can play with ratios of beans, kraut, and broth, but none of them should be the defining ingredient. It's not a bean soup or a sauerkraut soup; it is its own thing. If you aren't using good heirlooms, like our Royal Corona beans, for this recipe, the flavor won't be right. If you don't have homemade sauerkraut on hand, use a trusted brand. (There are lots of very good artisan sauerkraut makers and even some good commercial brands, if you don't want to make your own.).* —Steve*

# SAUERKRAUT BEAN SOUP

3 tablespoons extra-virgin olive oil

½ of a yellow onion, peeled and diced

3 garlic cloves, peeled and thinly sliced

1 carrot, peeled and diced

1 celery stalk, diced

1 teaspoon dried thyme

2 cups cooked Rancho Gordo Alubia Blanca, Royal Corona, or other white bean, cooked as directed on page 22, then drained

2 cups bean broth, vegetable broth, or a combination

2 cups sauerkraut, drained well

Salt and freshly ground pepper

In a large saucepan, warm the olive oil over medium heat. Add the onion and garlic; cook, stirring, until soft and translucent, about 5 minutes. Add the carrot and celery; cook until soft, about 10 minutes. Add the thyme and cook for 1 minute.

Add the beans, broth, and sauerkraut; stir gently to combine. Simmer until the soup is thoroughly hot, about 10 minutes. Sauerkraut can be very salty, so check before adjusting seasoning. Ladle the soup into individual bowls, and serve with crusty bread.

*Serves 4–6*

**SAUERKRAUT** is fun to make at home. If you have one of our wooden bean-mashers (*machacadoras*), you can use it to mash the cabbage before fermentation.

*This soup is our version of Marcella Hazan's classic minestrone, which you can make in a slow cooker or on the stovetop (see note, below). I believe your bag of Rancho Gordo Marcella cannellini beans would feel right at home among all the fresh vegetables.* —*Steve*

# SLOW COOKER MINESTRONE

*1 cup Rancho Gordo Marcella beans, picked over and rinsed*

*1 tablespoon plus ¼ cup extra-virgin olive oil (divided use)*

*2 garlic cloves, minced*

*1 sprig of fresh rosemary*

*2 tablespoons salted butter*

*1 onion, thinly sliced*

*2 large carrots, peeled and diced*

*2 celery stalks, diced*

*1 russet potato, peeled and diced*

*½ pound green beans, trimmed and halved*

*2 medium zucchini, cubed*

*2 cups shredded Savoy cabbage or kale*

*Parmesan rind (optional)*

*½ cup canned plum tomatoes, with their juice*

*Salt and pepper*

*⅓ cup grated Parmesan cheese*

Place the beans in the slow cooker and cover with about 3 inches of water. Add the garlic, rosemary, and 1 tablespoon olive oil. Put the lid on the slow cooker and cook the beans on high until almost tender, about 2 hours.

Meanwhile, in a large stockpot, warm the ¼ cup oil and the butter over medium-low heat. Add the onion; cook until soft and golden, about 10 minutes. Add the carrots and celery; cook for 2 minutes. Add the potatoes; cook for another 2 minutes. Add the green beans and zucchini; cook for 2 minutes more. Add the cabbage; cook until wilted, another 5 or so minutes.

Add the vegetables, cheese rind (if using), and tomatoes to the slow cooker; stir well and season with salt. Cover and continue to cook on high until the beans and vegetables are tender and the broth is flavorful, another 2–3 hours.

Just before serving, remove the cheese rind (if using). Swirl in the grated cheese; season with salt and pepper.

*Serves 6*

**STOVETOP METHOD** If you prefer to start with cooked beans and simmer the soup on the stovetop: After sautéeing all the vegetables as directed, add 6 cups vegetable broth, bean broth, and/or water, along with the tomatoes and cheese rind (if using). Cover the pot and simmer gently for about 2 hours. Add 2–3 cups cooked Marcella beans and simmer for another 30 minutes.

*The essence of Pasta e Fagioli is pasta and beans, simply dressed. The pasta provides the texture, the beans and aromatics provide the broth, and the cheese and olive oil provide a sense of luxury. As you cook the beans, make sure to maintain a generous amount of cooking liquid; it will be the basis for your sauce. I think it's worth it to splurge on artisanal pasta for this dish—Baia is my favorite brand.* —Steve

# VEGETARIAN PASTA E FAGIOLI

*1 tablespoon extra-virgin olive oil, plus more for drizzling*

*1 medium onion, finely chopped*

*1 celery stalk, finely chopped*

*1 carrot, peeled and minced*

*1 garlic clove, minced*

*½ teaspoon red pepper flakes*

*1 tablespoon tomato paste*

*1 tablespoon mushroom powder*

*3 cups cooked Rancho Gordo Royal Corona and/or Cranberry beans in their broth, cooked as directed on page 22*

*1 rosemary sprig*

*Salt and freshly ground pepper*

*1 pound Baia Organic Durum Wheat Ringlets (or other tubular pasta)*

*Pecorino or Parmesan cheese for serving*

In a saucepan, warm the olive oil over medium heat. Add the onion, celery, carrot, and garlic; cook until the vegetables are soft and the onion is just turning golden, about 5 minutes. Add the red pepper flakes, tomato paste, and mushroom powder. Cook until the paste is warmed and tomato and mushroom aromas fill the room, about 3 minutes.

Add 4 cups of the bean broth—if you don't have 4 cups, make up the difference with water or vegetable broth—and rosemary; add salt and pepper to taste. Continue cooking at a gentle simmer until the liquid has reduced a bit, about 15 minutes (longer if you want a less soupy dish).

Cook the pasta according to package directions; drain.

Add the drained pasta and cooked beans to the vegetable mixture; mix well. Gently simmer for a few minutes to let the flavors mingle.

Serve immediately with a splash of peppery extra-virgin olive oil. Pass a bowl of grated pecorino or Parmesan cheese for guests to help themselves.

*Serves 6*

**CRANBERRY BEANS** are called Borlotti in Italy. I can think of 10 variations and there are probably many more, but you're safe substituting Cranberry beans for any recipe calling for Borlotti.

# ASPARAGUS-BEAN NESTS FOR BREAKFAST

*2 cups cooked Rancho Gordo white beans in their broth (such as Cassoulet, Alubia Blanca, or Marcella), cooked as directed on page 22*

*4 very fresh eggs*

*White vinegar*

*1 bunch of slender asparagus, tough ends trimmed, roasted or blanched until tender*

*Italian-Style Salsa Verde (page 150)*

In a small saucepan, warm the beans over low heat.

Bring a pot of water to a simmer over medium-low heat. Add a small dash of vinegar. Crack the eggs individually into a ramekin or cup. Slowly tip each egg into the water, swirling a spoon around the egg a bit to help keep its shape. Repeat with remaining eggs. Let cook until the whites have set around the edges, about 3 minutes. Remove eggs with a slotted spoon and drain on a paper towel.

Arrange a few asparagus spears in a circle on each plate. Fill each nest with about ½ cup of beans. Top with a poached egg and a generous amount of salsa verde.

*Serves 4*

**SALSA VERDE** is easy and inexact—use your favorite fresh herbs and play around with the amounts to come up with your own version. Drizzle it over any bean and you'll be happy.

*This is what you might call a rustic showstopper. If you're making asparagus for dinner, make some extra to use in this dish for breakfast the next morning. It beats Corn Flakes, and it's easy enough to poach eggs and rearrange some leftovers on a plate.*   —*Steve*

*You may have a stick of hard cinnamon on hand and you may be tempted to try it in this recipe, but please don't. You need the softer cinnamon called canela, also known as true cinnamon. Tomatoes spiced with soft canela are rich and warm; hard cinnamon has a brash flavor that works better for morning pastries and cookies than savory sauces. If you have leftover tomato sauce, you can thin it with some broth to make a soup or poach an egg. —Steve*

# FLAGEOLET BEANS IN TOMATO SAUCE

*2 cups cooked Rancho Gordo Flageolet beans in their broth, cooked as directed on page 22*

*3 white or yellow onion slices (skins can be left on)*

*2 garlic cloves, unpeeled*

*1 stick Rancho Gordo Canela (true cinnamon)*

*3–4 whole peeled tomatoes (canned is fine), and about ¼ cup of their juice*

*1 teaspoon dried Mexican oregano, preferably Rancho Gordo Oregano Indio*

*Vegetable broth, if needed*

*2 tablespoons extra-virgin olive oil*

*Salt*

*Chopped flat-leaf parsley for garnish*

*More olive oil and lemon wedges for serving (optional)*

In a small saucepan, warm the beans over low heat.

On a comal or cast-iron skillet, roast the onion slices and garlic over medium heat until soft, about 10 minutes, turning occasionally to avoid burning. Remove onion and garlic from the pan; set aside. Toast the canela on the comal, turning often, until fragrant, about 2 minutes; remove from heat and set aside. Peel the onions and garlic when cool enough to handle.

In a blender, puree the tomatoes, tomato juice, oregano, onions, and garlic. Add a little broth if the blades get stuck.

In a large skillet, warm the olive oil over medium heat. Add the tomato mixture and toasted canela, stirring constantly. Raise heat to medium-high and keep stirring until the mixture thickens, about 15 minutes. Season with salt and remove the canela. You can add a little broth or water if the sauce is too thick.

For each serving, pour some sauce into a bowl and gently ladle the cooked beans into the center. Top with parsley. Serve as-is, or allow guests to drizzle their servings with olive oil and lemon.

*Serves 2–4*

*Flageolet beans are an odd variety. They have a thick skin that's somehow delicate at the same time. They're also mild enough to take on whatever flavors you give them. I cook them simply, with a bay leaf, and salt them once they start to get soft. Conventional wisdom says to dress beans while they're still warm, but I had a hunch that I wanted to toss them with a vinaigrette after they'd cooled. I wanted two distinct flavors: Beans and lemons, not lemony beans. Of course you can make the dressing in a blender or food processor, or just whisk the ingredients, but I prefer the drama of a mortar and pestle. Don't forget to stir in some chopped fresh parsley at the end. It's not just for color.* —Steve

# FLAGEOLET BEANS WITH LEMON DRESSING

*1 garlic clove, peeled*

*Salt*

*1½ teaspoons fresh thyme*

*3 tablespoons fresh lemon juice*

*About ¼ cup extra-virgin olive oil*

*3 cups cooked Rancho Gordo Flageolet beans, cooked as directed on page 22, then drained*

*Chopped flat-leaf parsley for garnish*

Using a mortar and pestle, pound the garlic with the salt and thyme. Add the lemon juice; mash well. Drizzle the olive oil into the mortar; mix until the sauce is emulsified. Adjust the oil-to-acid ratio as you see fit; this should be a bright dish.

Place the beans in a serving bowl and gently toss with the vinaigrette. Top with chopped parsley and serve.

*Serves 2–4 as a side dish*

**MEYER LEMONS** will make a sweeter, more floral vinaigrette than regular lemons.

*Canned tomatoes are tricky. I believe the quality used to be better. I do find that whole peeled tomatoes fare better than the diced variety. Their cans also seem to have more tomatoes and less liquid. Of course, you could adapt this recipe to use fresh, in-season tomatoes but I prefer to eat them raw during the brief window that they are at their best. This sauce is simple and delicious, but keep in mind that the beans should be the star—the sauce is just a supporting player.* —Steve

# ROYAL CORONA BEANS IN CREAMY TOMATO SAUCE

*2–4 cups cooked Rancho Gordo Royal Corona beans in their broth, cooked as directed on page 22*

*One 28-ounce can whole peeled Roma tomatoes*

*2 tablespoons olive oil*

*2 garlic cloves, minced*

*½ of a yellow onion, chopped*

*1 carrot, peeled and finely chopped*

*1 celery stalk, finely chopped*

*1 teaspoon salt*

*¼ cup vegetable broth*

*½ cup dry white wine*

*¼ cup heavy cream*

*Chopped flat-leaf parsley or basil for garnish*

*Extra-virgin olive oil for drizzling*

In a small saucepan, warm the beans over low heat.

Drain the tomatoes, reserving their liquid. Roughly chop the tomatoes; set aside.

In a large skillet, warm the olive oil over medium-high heat. Add the garlic, onion, carrot, and celery; cook until soft, 8–10 minutes, stirring occasionally. Add the salt, the tomatoes, and their liquid; cook for another 10 minutes. Add the broth and wine; cook for 5 minutes more. Reduce heat to low; add the cream and gently cook another 5 minutes. Check seasonings and add more salt, if necessary.

Ladle the beans into serving bowls and top each bowl with the sauce. Top with herbs and finish with a drizzle of olive oil.

*Serves 2–4*

**HEAVY CREAM** helps round out the flavors in the sauce, but you just want a touch. The beans provide plenty of indulgence.

*A friend told me about a recipe from Yotam Ottolenghi's cookbook,* Plenty, *with lima beans fried in butter and served with a tangle of wilted greens and soft cheese. I couldn't wait to try it. Here is my version. I used Rancho Gordo Stardust Dipping Powder as a seasoning, but if you don't have any on hand (you should!) you can use chile powder or even sumac, which is what Ottolenghi calls for in his original recipe.* —Julia

# FRIED WHITE LIMA BEANS WITH WILTED GREENS

*3 tablespoons olive oil, plus more for drizzling*

*3 tablespoons salted butter*

*4 cups cooked Rancho Gordo Large White Lima beans, cooked as directed on page 22, then drained and tossed with olive oil*

*4 green onions, sliced lengthwise into thin ribbons*

*1 garlic clove, minced*

*2–3 teaspoons Rancho Gordo Stardust Dipping Powder, chile powder, or sumac*

*4 cups baby arugula or baby spinach*

*Coarse sea salt*

*Zest and juice of one lemon*

*3 ounces goat cheese*

In a large skillet, warm about a tablespoon each of butter and oil over medium-high heat. Add enough beans to make a single layer in the pan. Let the beans fry, undisturbed, for a minute or two, then gently flip them and cook until golden and blistered on both sides.

Transfer the first batch of beans to a large bowl; repeat with the remaining butter, oil, and beans.

When you are done with the last batch of beans, add a splash of oil to the pan and then the green onions, garlic, Stardust, and arugula. Cook, stirring, until the greens are slightly wilted, about 2 minutes. Transfer the greens to the bowl of fried beans. Stir gently, then add salt, lemon zest, and lemon juice to taste.

Crumble cheese over the top, add a drizzle of olive oil, and serve.

*Serves 4*

**LIMA BEANS,** I've heard, got the nickname butter beans because they were often fried in butter. Now I know why! Make sure you fry the beans in batches so they can form a single layer in the pan. Don't fuss with them too much as they fry, or else you will end up with a pile of mashed beans.

*This recipe comes from a friend of a friend, whose family is from the island of Crete. Its simplicity embodies what I love about Mediterranean cooking. Don't be shy with the olive oil—you want the ingredients to be swimming in it. I think Royal Corona beans would work well in this dish, too.   —Julia*

# GREEK-STYLE BAKED WHITE LIMA BEANS

*½ cup olive oil (divided use)*

*1 large carrot, peeled and finely chopped*

*1 celery stalk, finely chopped*

*½ of an onion, finely chopped*

*2 tablespoons tomato paste*

*½ pound Rancho Gordo Large White Lima beans, cooked as directed on page 22, then drained*

*1 large tomato, chopped*

*3 tablespoons minced fresh dill*

*Salt and freshly ground pepper*

*Feta cheese (optional)*

Preheat the oven to 350°F.

In a large skillet, warm 2 tablespoons of the olive oil over medium heat. Add the carrot, celery, and onion; sauté until the vegetables are soft, about 5 minutes. Stir in the tomato paste.

In a large baking dish, combine the sautéed vegetables, beans, tomato, and remaining olive oil. Sprinkle with salt, pepper, and dill. Add feta, if desired.

Bake until the beans are soft and creamy, about 30 minutes.

*Serves 4*

**MIREPOIX** is a fancy name for carrots, celery, and onion that have been finely chopped. I use it as a trusted seasoning base for just about any dish using heirloom beans.

*My love of Cassoulet led me to this quick, delicious dish. For some customers, a pound of beans can be intimidating. What to do with all the leftovers from that first simple pot? Even I can struggle if I've had no dinner guests. This is an easy dish. I've tried it with just beans and no vegetables and it's too heavy. The onions and fennel are perfect, but I imagine slow-cooked leeks would work just as well.* —Steve

# WHITE BEAN GRATIN

5 tablespoons extra-virgin olive
oil (divided use)

2 medium fennel bulbs, outer
layers removed, cored and thinly
sliced

1 yellow onion, chopped

2 garlic cloves, minced

2 cups cooked Rancho Gordo
white beans in their broth (such
as Flageolet, Marcella, Alubia
Blanca, Cassoulet, or Royal
Corona), cooked as directed on
page 22

½ cup bread crumbs

1 teaspoon dried thyme

In a large skillet, warm 3 tablespoons of the olive oil over medium heat. Add the fennel, onion, and garlic; sauté until soft and well-cooked, 15–20 minutes. Gently stir in the beans and remove from heat.

Preheat the oven to 375°F.

In a small bowl, mix the remaining 2 tablespoons olive oil, bread crumbs, and thyme.

In a 9-inch gratin dish, first add the onion-bean mixture. Add enough of the reserved bean-cooking liquid so that the liquid rises just halfway up the beans. Top with the breadcrumb mixture.

Bake until the bread crumbs are brown and the liquid is bubbling, about 20 minutes.

*Serves 6–8*

**BREAD CRUMBS** are a staple in my kitchen. For store-bought bread crumbs, I prefer Japanese panko. If you have stale bread lying around, you can make your own: Pulse the bread slices in a food processor until fine crumbs form, then spread the crumbs on a baking sheet and bake at 350°F until dry, about 10 minutes.

# ALUBIA BLANCA BEANS WITH MORELS AND ROSEMARY

*1 pound Rancho Gordo Alubia Blanca, Cassoulet, or Royal Corona beans, picked over and soaked (see page 22)*

*1 bay leaf*

*¼ of a white onion, peeled and diced*

*6 garlic cloves, peeled (divided use)*

*1 cup dried morel mushrooms*

*3 tablespoons coarsely chopped fresh rosemary*

*2 teaspoons sea salt, plus more for bean cooking*

*¼ cup extra-virgin olive oil*

In a large pot, combine the beans, their soaking water, bay leaf, onion, and 2 whole garlic cloves. Add more water if needed to cover the beans by about 2 inches of water. Raise heat to high and allow the water to maintain a full boil for 15 minutes. Reduce heat to low, letting the beans gently simmer until soft, 1½–2 hours. Salt as soon as the beans start getting soft, allowing time for the beans to absorb the salt.

Meanwhile, in a medium bowl, cover the mushrooms in hot but not boiling water (see note). Use a small plate to keep the mushrooms submerged; soak for about 20 minutes. Remove the mushrooms, gently swishing them in the soaking liquid to remove any remaining grit, and slice them into rings. Strain the soaking liquid through a fine-mesh sieve and save it for another use.

Chop the remaining 4 garlic cloves with the rosemary and 2 teaspoons of salt until you have a coarse mixture.

In a skillet, warm the oil over medium heat; add the rosemary mixture, stirring well and cooking until the garlic is golden and fragrant, about 5 minutes. Add the mushrooms; cook another 5 minutes. Watch the mushrooms carefully to make sure they don't overcook and get mushy.

Ladle the beans into serving bowls; top each bowl with 2 tablespoons of the mushroom mixture. Allow guests to stir the topping into the beans.

*Serves 4–6*

**DRIED MORELS** aren't as gritty as porcini and other mushrooms, and quality mushroom brands like Wine Forest don't tend to be gritty, so you may be able to skip the rinsing step. Don't be tempted to use hot tap water for mushroom soaking—it's better to heat the water on the stove.

*My friend and neighbor Connie Green is a forager who's very generous with her mushrooms. I've had such a good time figuring out delicious things to do with them. So far, my favorite method has been to sauté them with heaps of garlic, rosemary, and salt using lots of good olive oil. Drizzling this mixture over mild, white beans may not sound very exciting, but it's been a huge hit with my dining pals. You don't want to cook the beans together with the morels. Rather than blended flavors, we're going for layers. And really, it couldn't be easier... especially if you've made your beans ahead of time. This is a good gateway dish if you're looking to cut down the amount of meat in your diet. It's substantial without being heavy, and I can't imagine anyone leaving the table in anything less than a good mood.* —Steve

# QUICK IDEAS No Recipe Needed

**MARCELLA BEANS** topped with extra-virgin olive oil and fresh sage

**CASSOULET BEANS** mixed with ricotta cheese and steamed spinach

# QUICK IDEAS No Recipe Needed

**FLAGEOLET BEANS** with roasted bell pepper, capers, and vinaigrette on toast

**ALUBIA BLANCA BEANS** with bean broth, broccoli rabe, and a poached egg

*Chapter 2*
# MEDIUM-BODIED BEANS

The Cranberry bean represents this group best. It's dense and bold but mild and velvety. Good heirloom Cranberry beans have thin skins but retain their shape, releasing a perfect bean broth. It's obvious to use them in soups, taking advantage of their pot liquor, but they also shine in refried beans, Pasta e Fagioli, and salads.

Don't overlook Yellow Eye and Mayocoba beans for creamy soups, dips, and refried beans.

These beans are among the best and my favorite recipe is this: Serve hot and drizzle extra-virgin olive oil over them. *Ta-da!*

*This is a great dish for entertaining because you can prepare the spread in advance and assemble the toasts right before serving. Or, serve them with a simple salad for a quick and satisfying weeknight dinner. I used Cranberry beans but I think any medium-bodied beans, or even white beans, would work.* —Julia

# CRANBERRY BEANS AND RAPINI ON TOAST

1 small bunch broccoli rabe (rapini)

1 tablespoon olive oil

Salt

1 or 2 garlic cloves, minced

½ cup pitted olives (preferably Kalamata)

1 tablespoon red wine vinegar

Zest and juice of 1 lemon

¼ cup extra-virgin olive oil, plus more for drizzling

Pinch of red pepper flakes (optional)

2 cups cooked Rancho Gordo Cranberry or Yellow Eye beans, cooked as directed on page 22, then drained

Slices of fresh rustic bread, lightly toasted

Shaved Parmesan cheese for serving

Trim the tough ends of the broccoli rabe, then peel the remaining stems with a vegetable peeler. Rinse well. Bring a large pot of salted water to a boil. Add the broccoli rabe; cook until tender but not mushy, about 10 minutes. Drain, then roughly chop.

In a skillet, warm 1 tablespoon oil over medium-low heat. Add the garlic; cook until fragrant, about 1 minute. Add the broccoli rabe; toss and stir until coated with oil and garlic, about 10 minutes.

In the bowl of a food processor, combine the olives, vinegar, lemon zest and juice, ¼ cup olive oil, and red pepper flakes (if using); process until smooth. Add the beans and broccoli rabe; pulse just until combined but still chunky. Add salt to taste.

Smear a dollop of the bean-rapini mixture on each bread slice. Drizzle with additional olive oil and dust with cheese.

*Serves 2 as a main dish, or 8 as an appetizer*

**BROCCOLI RABE/RAPINI** is also delicious roughly chopped, tossed with oil and salt, and roasted on a sheet pan. Roast at 450°F for 7 minutes, shake the pan, then roast 5 minutes more until the leaves are crisp and the stalks are soft.

# FAGIOLI ALLA GLORIA

*2 cups cooked Rancho Gordo Cranberry beans, cooked as directed on page 22, then drained*

*1 shallot, very thinly sliced*

*1 small fennel bulb, trimmed and cored, sliced very thinly on a mandoline (fronds reserved for garnish)*

*2 garlic cloves, thinly sliced*

*A generous drizzle of the best extra-virgin olive oil*

*Champagne vinegar*

*Zest and juice of 1 Meyer lemon*

*Salt and freshly ground pepper*

*Toasted pumpkin seeds for garnish*

In a serving bowl, combine the beans, shallot, fennel, garlic, olive oil, vinegar, lemon juice, and zest. Gently mix the ingredients to combine. Add salt and pepper to taste.

If possible, let sit for an hour or two before serving to let the flavors mingle. Sprinkle with pumpkin seeds and fennel fronds just before serving.

*Serves 4 as a side dish*

*A million years ago, I took Italian lessons from a wonderful teacher named Gloria. She was very funny and yet a little reserved. I think my interest in Italian pop music amused and confused her. Well, it turns out she's still funny and a little reserved, and I know my interest in beans amuses and confuses her. Gloria Lynch is now an artist in Colorado. She sent me an email with her take on Borlotti or Cranberry beans; it's simple and very good!* —Steve

*I used to say that anything made with lemons is always better with limes. Ah, youth! Lemons are completely different. Italian barley is nutty and chewy, but you could easily replace it with farro, wheat berries, wild rice, or even brown rice. The next time you make one of these grains, prepare some extra and toss with leftover beans and herbs.* —Steve

# CRANBERRY BEAN AND BARLEY SALAD WITH CAPERS AND HERBS

¼ cup olive oil

¼ cup lemon juice

1½ cups cooked Rancho Gordo Cranberry beans, cooked as directed on page 22, then drained

3 cups cooked Italian barley, farro, or hard red wheat berries

2 green onions, white parts only, thinly sliced

½ cup chopped flat-leaf parsley

½ cup chopped basil

Salt and freshly ground pepper

¼ cup salt-packed capers, fried (optional; see note)

In a serving bowl, whisk together the olive oil and lemon juice. Gently fold in the cooked beans, cooked grains, green onions, and herbs. Season with salt and pepper and top with the fried capers, if using. Serve at room temperature.

*Serves 4*

**SALT-PACKED CAPERS** need to be rinsed and soaked for a few hours before you use them, but that's a very small problem. After they've soaked, squeeze them dry and pat with a paper towel. At this point, you can add them to your dish or take it a step further: Fry them in olive oil until they're just crisp and then let them rest on a paper towel until you're ready to use.

# YELLOW EYE BEAN AND KALE SOUP

1 tablespoon olive oil, plus more for drizzling

1 garlic clove, minced

1 large carrot, peeled and chopped

1 small bunch Tuscan kale, leaves stripped from the stems and sliced into thin ribbons

1½ cups cooked Rancho Gordo Yellow Eye beans in their broth, cooked as directed on page 22

1 sprig fresh rosemary

4–6 cups vegetable broth

Grated lemon zest

Red pepper flakes (optional)

Salt and freshly ground pepper

Thin slices of baguette, toasted and cut into small croutons

Grated Parmesan cheese for serving

In a large saucepan, warm the olive oil over medium-low heat. Add the garlic; cook until fragrant, about 1 minute. Add the carrot; cook until softened, about 3 minutes. Add the kale ribbons; toss until they are coated with oil and garlic. Add the beans, rosemary, and about 6 cups total of bean-cooking liquid and vegetable broth. Raise heat to medium-high; simmer until the kale is tender, about 15 minutes. Remove the rosemary sprig and stir in lemon zest, red pepper flakes (if using), salt, and pepper to taste.

Top each serving with croutons, a drizzle of olive oil and some freshly grated cheese.

*Serves 4*

---

**FRESH ROSEMARY** is one of my favorite herbs to cook with, but too much can overpower a dish. I often throw a big sprig of rosemary into the pot when I'm cooking beans. It infuses the bean broth with a rich flavor and helps create a great base for soups and stews.

*Somehow, kale has become a very trendy ingredient. Kale Caesar salads, kale chips, kale smoothies—kale is everywhere you look! I very much enjoy the flavor of kale so I'm all for this trend. I especially love it in a simple soup like this. Any hearty green, such as chard, collards, or spinach, would also work.* —Julia

*In our house, we call this Fergie Salad, named after a friend who has a gift for creating amazing salad dishes. One time, I added some leftover beans to Fergie's usual combination, and it was a hit, especially because the beans transformed it from a side dish into a more substantial meal. I love this as a cold salad, but you can also sauté the vegetables in the oil until soft (throw in some chopped zucchini, too), then add the fresh basil and mozzarella before serving.* —Julia

# SANTA MARIA PINQUITO BEAN SALAD WITH CORN, TOMATOES, AND BASIL

*1 pint cherry or grape tomatoes, halved*

*1 small bunch fresh basil, julienned or chopped*

*2–3 tablespoons extra-virgin olive oil*

*2 tablespoons balsamic vinegar or Rancho Gordo Pineapple Vinegar*

*Salt and freshly ground pepper*

*2 cups cooked Rancho Gordo Santa Maria Pinquito beans, cooked as directed on page 22, then drained*

*Cooked corn kernels from 3 ears (try grilling the corn)*

*8 ounces fresh mozzarella balls, halved or quartered*

Combine the tomatoes, basil, oil, vinegar, and salt and pepper in a salad bowl. Refrigerate for 15 minutes or so to marry the flavors.

Add the beans, corn, and cheese and stir gently to combine. Season with salt and pepper, and serve.

*Serves 2–4 as a main dish*

# BEAN AND FARRO SOUP

¼ cup extra virgin olive oil, plus a little more for drizzling

1 medium yellow onion, finely chopped

1 large or 2 small carrots, peeled and finely chopped

1 celery stalk, finely chopped

2 garlic cloves, minced

1½ cups Rancho Gordo Emmer (farro medio)

6 cups liquid (vegetable broth, bean broth, or a combination)

1 cup cooked Rancho Gordo Cranberry, Alubia Blanca, or Marcella beans, cooked as directed on page 22

Sea salt

Freshly ground pepper

¼ cup chopped celery leaves (or flat-leaf parsley)

In a medium saucepan, warm the olive oil over medium heat. Add the onion, carrot, and celery; cook until soft, about 10 minutes. Add the garlic and farro; continue cooking for 2 minutes more, stirring frequently. Slowly add the liquid; reduce to a simmer and cook until farro is tender, stirring frequently, 30–45 minutes.

Add the beans and more liquid, if desired; season with salt and pepper. Cook until the beans are warmed through.

Serve in warmed bowls, garnished with celery leaves or parsley and a drizzle of olive oil.

*Serves 4*

*Good beans, good grains, good olive oil, and some garlic. That's the beauty of simple cooking. This a classic dish, inspired by a recipe from Pamela Sheldon Jones' Cucina Povera. On the surface, it's classic Tuscan peasant cooking, but it's really about the genius of the Italian kitchen. Take something good and keep paring it down to its most basic. You can easily use a white bean here (as I did when I took this photo), but I love the velvety Cranberry Bean texture and broth, especially with the farro.* —Steve

*I first heard of Margaret Roach when I saw her singing the praises of Rancho Gordo Cranberry beans on national television. Of course, I instantly fell in love with her! She was showing Martha Stewart how to make this very dish. She was kind enough to share the recipe with us and it's been very popular.* —Steve

# MARGARET ROACH'S RATHER FAMOUS BAKED BEANS

*1 pound Rancho Gordo Cranberry or Yellow Eye beans, picked over and soaked (see page 22)*

*Extra-virgin olive oil*

*2 medium onions, cut into quarters*

*¼ cup molasses (preferably Wholesome Sweeteners organic)*

*¼ cup dark amber maple syrup*

*4 tablespoons grainy mustard*

*4–6 Italian-style paste tomatoes, roughly chopped (or substitute another tomato variety, canned tomatoes, or even some red sauce)*

*Boiling water*

Preheat the oven to 350°F.

In a large saucepan, add the beans and enough water to cover beans by about 2 inches. Bring the liquid to a hard boil over high heat; cook 10–15 minutes. Simmer the beans until barely tender, about 30 minutes.

Coat a large, lidded, ovenproof pot—such as a Dutch oven, casserole, or ceramic bean pot—with a splash of olive oil. Lay the quartered onions in the bottom.

Drain the beans and place in a large bowl. Add the molasses, maple syrup, mustard, and tomatoes; toss to coat. Pour the bean mixture over the onions in the pot. Add enough boiling water to cover beans by about an inch.

Cover and bake until the beans are tender, about 2 hours, adjusting the oven temperature to keep the beans at a lazy bubble. Remove the lid occasionally and check the water level, adding more hot water to keep beans submerged.

Once the beans reach an almost-ready tenderness, uncover the pot and raise heat to 375°F. Continue to cook for another hour or so, reducing the liquid to a thick brown syrup, stirring a few times to combine. During this last phase, adjust for sweetness, salt, and tomato flavor, balancing the maple-to-molasses ratio to taste.

*Serves 6–8 as a side dish*

*Everyone seems to be in love with tacos. They are wonderful, but why neglect tostadas? If you have a good, crunchy tostada and a layer of refried beans, you have the foundation for something great and the possibilities are endless. To puree the refried beans, I use a wooden bean masher, or* machacadora. *Of course, I would have such a specialized tool, but odds are you won't. You can use a potato masher instead. Or, you can purchase your very own* machacadora *from Rancho Gordo.* —Steve

# TOSTADAS WITH REFRIED BEANS

*2 tablespoons corn oil or olive oil, plus 1 cup for frying*

*1 small white onion, very thinly sliced*

*3 cups cooked Rancho Gordo brown beans in their broth (such as Mayocoba, Pinto, or Rebosero), cooked as directed on page 22*

*8 corn tortillas*

FOR THE REFRIED BEANS:

In a skillet, warm 2 tablespoons oil over medium-high heat. Add the onion; cook until soft. Add the beans and their broth; bring to a simmer. Mash some beans and onion together to make a paste, continuing until beans are mostly mashed and onions have disappeared. When you can see the bottom of the pan as you drag the masher through the beans, you're done.

FOR THE TOSTADAS:

In a skillet, warm 1 cup of oil over medium heat. Fry 1 or 2 tortillas at a time, flipping once, until firm. Remove and drain on paper towels; set aside.

TO SERVE:

Arrange all of your ingredients and let diners create their own tostadas.

*Serves 4*

**TOPPINGS** Salsa Fresca, guacamole, Mexican Salsa Verde (page 151), Mushroom Carnitas (page 117), pickled vegetables, shredded lettuce, sautéed greens, cotija cheese, crema mexicana or sour cream, and/or lime wedges.

*A savory pudding might sound odd, but this recipe is a keeper. Some might like it as a side dish, but I think it's a great, simple main course. It's light and substantial at the same time, and nothing like you might imagine until you actually make it. I've tried many cheeses and I've ended up liking a mix of Swiss and Parmesan. However, you can play around, since it's just a little cheese for topping. This is a bean dish, not a cheesy, gooey pizza.* —Steve

# SAVORY BEAN AND EGG PUDDING

1 tablespoon salted butter, softened to room temperature

2 cups cooked Rancho Gordo
beans (such as Cranberry, Moro,
or Royal Corona), cooked as directed on page 22, then drained

2 large eggs

2 garlic cloves, chopped

½ cup heavy whipping cream

Salt and freshly ground pepper

1 tablespoon grated Swiss cheese

2 tablespoons grated Parmesan
cheese

Preheat oven to 350°F. Grease a small gratin or baking dish with
the butter.

In a mixing bowl, combine the beans, eggs, garlic, cream, salt, and
pepper. Puree the mixture with an immersion blender until smooth
(or use a blender or food processor).

Pour the mixture into the buttered dish; top with cheeses. Bake for
20–30 minutes, until the top is brown and the center is set. (If the
center is still liquid, keep baking for another 10 minutes.)

Serves 2

**BEAN TYPES** I've made this recipe several times and used a different bean each time, and I encourage you to do
the same. White and medium-bodied beans are prettiest but dark beans add more interesting flavors.

*Chile Relleno literally means stuffed chile. It doesn't mean it has to be stuffed with cheese or meat, egg-battered, and then deep-fried. I've stuffed them with quinoa and beans and they were a hit with guests. Think of them like Italian stuffed peppers, with a richer, denser poblano chile flavor. For a cheesier dish, replace some of the cotija with Oaxaca-style string cheese or mozzarella.* —Steve

# BAKED CHILES RELLENOS WITH YELLOW INDIAN WOMAN BEANS

*1 cup cooked Rancho Gordo Yellow Indian Woman beans (or Tepary beans), cooked as directed on page 22, then drained*

*½ cup chopped white onion*

*1 cup cotija cheese, grated*

*½ cup crema mexicana (or sour cream thinned with milk)*

*2 tablespoons pureed chipotle chiles in adobo sauce*

*Salt and pepper*

*4 whole poblano chiles, charred, peeled, and seeded (see page 148)*

Preheat oven to 350°F.

In a large mixing bowl, gently combine the cooked beans, onion, half the cheese, half the crema, the chipotle chiles, salt, and pepper.

Fill each poblano chile with about a quarter of the bean mixture; place the stuffed chiles on an ungreased baking sheet in a single layer.

Drizzle the remaining crema over the chiles and top with the remaining cheese. Bake for 15 minutes. Serve while warm.

*Serves 4*

# QUICK IDEAS No Recipe Needed

**BEAN FLOWER QUESADILLA**

**SMASHED YELLOW INDIAN WOMAN BEANS** with macerated tomatoes and herbs on toast

*Chapter 3*
# DARK & HEARTY BEANS

In some regions of the world, "beans" means black beans. They have a rich, fudgy texture and inky bean broth that needs little more to make a soup. It's easy to think of them for beans and rice, Brazilian feijoada, or Oaxacan enfrijoladas, but don't ignore them for salads or nachos.

But there is so much more to this category than black beans: dark, pinto-like Rio Zape beans, large purple and black runner beans (known as Ayo-cotes in Mexico), Christmas Limas, red beans, and more.

*Rio Zape beans continue to be one of my favorites. In honor of the Super Bowl, which I try but fail to find interesting, I came up with this dip. I know a bean dip seems like an obvious thing for me, but I'd just never gotten around to it before. You can use any of our hot sauces in place of the Felicidad.* —Steve

# CREAMY RIO ZAPE BEAN DIP

*2 tablespoons extra-virgin olive oil*

*½ of a yellow onion, sliced very thin*

*2 garlic cloves, minced*

*1 cup cooked Rancho Gordo Rio Zape beans in their broth, cooked as directed on page 22*

*2 tablespoons Rancho Gordo Felicidad hot sauce*

*2 tablespoons sour cream*

*2 tablespoons minced cilantro*

In a skillet, warm the olive oil over medium-low heat. Add the onion and garlic; cook until soft, about 10 minutes. Add the beans and their broth, the hot sauce, and sour cream.

Remove from heat and blend the mixture with an immersion blender until smooth (or let cool slightly and process in batches in a blender or food processor). Chill for at least 2 hours.

When ready to serve, spoon the dip into a serving bowl or platter; sprinkle cilantro over the top. Serve with crudites, crackers, or chips for dipping.

*Serves 6–8*

**CRUDITES** can be any type of sliced, fresh vegetable. It's fun to serve something unexpected on a crudite platter, like purple heirloom carrots, mini bell peppers, or quartered lemon cucumbers.

# BLACK BEAN SALAD WITH RADISHES, CELERY, AND ONION

1 teaspoon salt

1 teaspoon Mexican oregano, preferably Rancho Gordo Oregano Indio

2 tablespoons Rancho Gordo Pineapple Vinegar

¼ cup extra-virgin olive oil

1½ cups cooked Rancho Gordo Midnight Black beans, cooked as directed on page 22, then drained

4 large radishes, thinly sliced with a mandoline

1 celery stalk, thinly sliced with a mandoline

½ of a small red onion, thinly sliced with a mandoline

Handful of flat-leaf parsley, chopped

¼ cup crumbled goat cheese

In a serving bowl, whisk together the salt, oregano, vinegar, and olive oil. Add the beans, radishes, celery, onion, and parsley; toss to combine. Taste and adjust seasoning. Sprinkle with crumbled goat cheese and serve.

Serves 4

**RED ONION** I love the taste and crunch of raw red onion, but it can be too intense for some people. If you want to tame the flavor, soak the slices in ice water for about 10 minutes, then drain and add to the salad. You can also soak them in vinegar, lemon juice, or lime juice for added flavor.

*In this salad, I took some cooked Rancho Gordo Midnight Black beans and tossed them with mandoline-sliced radishes, celery, and red onion, plus some parsley. Then I crumbled some goat cheese (not much!) into the mix. It helps if the cheese is very cold or it might be too soft to crumble. For me, this is heaven. I am happy to eat nothing but a simple bowl of this salad for dinner, maybe with good bread. If you don't have Midnight beans on hand, I would try Domingo Rojo, San Franciscano, or even Santa Maria Pinquito beans, realizing that the salad will be just as good, but somewhat different.* —Steve

*Confession: My lunch often consists of a premade, packaged salad from the grocery store. Because, after packing two kid lunches every night, I rarely have the energy to pack something for myself. This recipe is based on one of my favorite premade salads. I am hopeful that someday I will have time to pack myself a homemade lunch, and when that day comes, this will certainly be on the menu.* —Julia

# DOMINGO ROJO BEAN AND QUINOA SALAD WITH PUMPKIN SEEDS

*1½ cups cooked quinoa*

*1½ cups cooked Rancho Gordo Domingo Rojo beans, cooked as directed on page 22, then drained*

*2 large carrots, peeled and shredded*

*4 cups shredded Romaine lettuce or mixed greens*

*Green Sauce (page 113)*

*¼ cup toasted pumpkin seeds*

*1 avocado, cubed (optional)*

In a serving bowl, combine the quinoa, beans, carrots, and lettuce. Dress with a generous amount of the Green Sauce (enough to saturate all of the ingredients); toss to combine. Divide among serving bowls and top with the pumpkin seeds and avocado, if using.

*Serves 4*

*I must sound like a broken record when I say that many of the best dishes were born from using up leftovers. At some point, someone had some stale tortillas, salsa, and a great imagination. Eggs make this dish more substantial but I almost prefer this dish without them, especially if the chile sauce is excellent.* —Steve

# CHILAQUILES WITH POACHED EGGS

For the chile sauce:

*4 ancho chiles*

*2 guajillo chiles*

*1 small onion, chopped*

*1 teaspoon dried Mexican oregano, preferably Rancho Gordo Oregano Indio*

*1–2 garlic cloves, peeled*

*1 tablespoon corn oil or extra-virgin olive oil*

*Vegetable broth or water*

*Salt*

*Sugar (optional)*

For the chilaquiles:

*4 fresh eggs*

*About 2 cups stale tortilla chips*

*1½ cups cooked Rancho Gordo Midnight Black beans, cooked as directed on page 22, then drained*

*Grated cotija cheese, crema mexicana, chopped fresh cilantro, and sliced avocado for serving*

Clean the chiles, then toast them on a dry skillet or comal over high heat for 3 minutes. Soak the toasted chiles in warm water for about 20 minutes. Place the rehydrated chiles in a blender with enough of the soaking liquid to keep the blades moving. Add the onion, oregano, and garlic; blend well.

In a large skillet, warm the oil over medium heat. Add the chile puree; fry for 5 minutes. Thin the sauce with broth or water; cook another 15 minutes or so. Add salt as needed, and a touch of sugar if the sauce is bitter.

Bring the sauce to a simmer and gently add the eggs, one at a time. Cook until the whites have set but the yolk is still runny, about 3 minutes. Remove the eggs with a slotted spoon and set aside on paper towels.

Add the tortilla chips and beans to the chile sauce and cook until the chips are soft and pliable, about 5 minutes.

Divide the tortilla pieces among two plates; top with grated cotija cheese and the poached eggs. Drizzle with a little crema, and top with cilantro and sliced avocado.

*Serves 2*

*This salad is heavy on the beans and cauliflower and light on the spinach. The key to its deliciousness is tossing it together while the beans and cauliflower are still warm. This will wilt the spinach a bit and help the flavors mingle. Any type of bean would work here, but I think a larger bean like Christmas Lima is best so it doesn't get lost in the mix.    —Julia*

# CHRISTMAS LIMA BEAN AND ROASTED CAULIFLOWER SALAD

*2–3 cups cooked Rancho Gordo Christmas Lima beans, cooked as directed on page 22, then drained*

*2 small (or 1 large) heads of cauliflower, cut into small florets (about 4 cups)*

*3 tablespoons plus ¼ cup extra-virgin olive oil (divided use)*

*Salt and freshly ground pepper*

*Juice of 1 large lemon*

*1 tablespoon grainy mustard*

*1 tablespoon honey*

*4 cups baby spinach*

*Grated Parmesan cheese*

In a small saucepan, warm the beans over low heat.

Preheat the oven to 400°F. Spread the cauliflower on a baking sheet; toss with 3 tablespoons olive oil and a generous amount of salt. Bake, stirring occasionally, until the cauliflower is deep golden brown and caramelized around the edges, about 20 minutes.

In a glass jar with a lid, combine the lemon juice, mustard, honey, ¼ cup olive oil, plus salt and pepper to taste. Cover the jar and shake until the dressing is smooth and creamy. Taste and adjust seasonings.

In a serving bowl, combine the spinach, beans, and warm cauliflower. Add the dressing and toss to combine. Taste and adjust seasonings again. Finish with grated cheese.

*Serves 4 as a main dish*

**FINISHING SALT** will enhance the flavors in a salad and, frankly, just make it taste better. I usually underseason my salad dressing and then sprinkle a finished salad with some flaky Maldon sea salt before serving.

*Who needs beef broth when you have rich, flavorful Christmas Lima bean broth? This is an indulgent dish, based on the classic French onion soup. You could easily make a dairy-free version by caramelizing the onions in olive oil and omitting the cheese.* —Julia

# CARAMELIZED ONION AND CHRISTMAS LIMA BEAN SOUP

*2 tablespoons salted butter*

*1 tablespoon extra-virgin olive oil*

*3 medium onions, thinly sliced*

*Salt and freshly ground pepper*

*1 teaspoon sugar*

*1 cup dry red wine*

*6 sprigs fresh thyme*

*1 bay leaf*

*2 cups cooked Rancho Gordo Christmas Lima beans, cooked as directed on page 22, then drained, plus 5 cups bean broth*

*8 slices sourdough baguette, toasted until crisp*

*1–1½ cups shredded Gruyere cheese*

In a large saucepan, melt the butter over medium heat. Add the oil and onions; cook until the onions are soft, stirring occasionally, about 10 minutes. Add the salt, pepper, and sugar. Reduce heat to low; continue to cook, stirring occasionally, until the onions are golden brown and caramelized, about 45 minutes.

Add the wine and raise heat to high. Cook until almost all liquid has evaporated, 8–10 minutes.

Wrap the thyme and bay leaf in cheesecloth, or tie with kitchen string. Add bean broth and the herb bundle to the pot with the onions. Bring to a boil, then reduce heat to medium-low; simmer until the broth is thick and flavorful, about 20 minutes. Stir in the beans and remove the herb bundle.

Preheat the broiler.

Place 4 ramekins or oven-safe bowls on a rimmed baking sheet, and divide the soup among the bowls. Top each serving of soup with two toasts. Divide the cheese among the servings, covering the bread and some of the soup. Carefully transfer the baking sheet to the oven and broil until the cheese is melted and bubbling, 4–6 minutes.

*Serves 4*

*Instead of discarding corncobs, use them to create a sweet broth with the essence of corn. Once you have the broth, you can create endless variations on this corn chowder. Here, creamy potatoes, black beans, and crunchy corn make a winning combination. Chopped zucchini or roasted poblano chiles would also be great additions. You could also puree some, or all, of the soup, if you prefer a smooth consistency.* —*Julia*

# BLACK BEAN, POTATO AND CORN CHOWDER

For the corn broth:

*4 corncobs, kernels removed and reserved*

*1 bay leaf*

*5 whole peppercorns*

For the chowder:

*2 tablespoons salted butter or olive oil*

*1 small onion, chopped*

*1 jalapeño chile, minced (optional)*

*3 medium waxy potatoes, cubed*

*Corn kernels from 4 ears*

*3 cups cooked Rancho Gordo Midnight Black beans (or other dark bean) in their broth, cooked as directed on page 22*

*Salt and pepper*

*Lime wedges and hot sauce for serving*

In a stockpot, combine the corncobs, bay leaf, peppercorns, and 2 quarts of water; bring to a boil over high heat. Reduce heat to low; simmer until the broth is sweet and flavorful, about 45 minutes. Remove from heat and let cool. Strain the broth and discard the solids. You should have about 6 cups.

In a large saucepan over medium-low heat, melt the butter. Add the onion; cook until soft, about 10 minutes. Add the jalapeño, if using; cook for another couple of minutes. Add the potatoes, corn kernels, and corn broth; bring to a boil over high heat. Reduce heat to low and simmer until the potatoes are tender, about 15 minutes. Stir in the beans; cook until warm. Season with salt and pepper.

Ladle into bowls and serve with lime wedges and hot sauce.

*Serves 4–6*

The hacienda that hosts much of the activities of our Rancho Gordo-Xoxoc Project was bustling with guests and meals during our last visit. This simple soup might seem more indulgent than it really is. Please don't try this with commodity beans. It won't work. A simple dish like this needs the best ingredients. Save your old tortillas and use them for this dish. They're better when they're a little stale and tend not to absorb much oil.   —Steve

# SOPA CAMPESINA

1 tablespoon extra-virgin olive oil

½ of a yellow onion, chopped

2 garlic cloves, minced

½ pound Rancho Gordo Rebosero beans, picked over and rinsed (see page 22)

Sea salt

3 corn tortillas, preferably a little stale, cut into very thin strips

Oil for frying

1 teaspoon Mexican oregano, preferably Rancho Gordo Oregano Indio

Limes for garnish

In a large pot, warm the olive oil over medium heat. Add the onion and garlic; cook until soft, about 10 minutes. Add the beans and enough water to cover beans by about 2 inches. Raise heat to high and bring the liquid to a hard boil over high heat; cook for 10–15 minutes. Reduce heat to low and allow beans to gently simmer. Make sure the beans are always covered by about 2 inches of liquid, adding hot water as needed.

After about an hour, the beans should begin to soften. Add a tablespoon of salt, and allow the beans to continue cooking until done. Total time will be between 90 minutes and 3 hours. If it's taking too long, raise the heat a bit.

While the beans are cooking, warm the oil in a skillet over medium-high heat. Fry the tortilla strips in the hot oil until crisp; drain on paper towels and salt generously.

When the beans are soft, adjust the seasoning to taste and add the teaspoon of oregano. Ladle into bowls and top with the tortilla strips. Serve with limes.

*Serves 2–4*

# CHILI SIN CARNE

1 tablespoon cumin seeds (or 1 teaspoon ground cumin)

5 cloves

2 whole allspice

4 tablespoons olive oil

⅓ to ½ cup Rancho Gordo 100% Pure Chile Powder

1 tablespoon dried Mexican oregano, preferably Rancho Gordo Mexican Oregano or Oregano Indio

1 teaspoon smoked Spanish paprika (optional)

1 tablespoon porcini mushroom powder (optional)

2 cups vegetable broth

8 cups cooked Rancho Gordo Ayocote Negro beans in their broth, cooked as directed on page 22

Sugar (optional)

4 zucchini, sliced in rounds

Fresh corn kernels from 3 ears

Sea salt

Lime wedges and Crème fraîche, for serving

Grind the cumin seeds, cloves, and allspice in a mortar or electric spice grinder. (If using ground cumin, add to the pot along with the ground spices below.)

In a large, heavy stockpot or Dutch oven, warm the olive oil over medium heat until it shimmers. Add the chile powder, stirring constantly, for 5 minutes. Add the ground spices, oregano, paprika, and porcini powder (if using). Mix thoroughly; continue cooking until you have a dense paste, about 3 minutes.

Add the vegetable broth very slowly, stirring constantly until well blended. Stir in the beans and their broth. Reduce heat to medium-low; simmer about 20 minutes, stirring occasionally. Add about a tablespoon of salt; cook for another 10 minutes. Taste and adjust seasoning, adding more salt, if needed. If the broth is bitter, add sugar to taste, a bit at a time. (Two teaspoons is more than enough.)

Continue simmering, stirring occasionally, until the chili starts to thicken and no grainy texture remains from the chile powder. Add the zucchini and corn; cook for another 15 minutes.

Serve with lime wedges and crème fraîche, if you like.

*Serves 6–8*

---

**SEASONINGS** I make this chili with both porcini powder and smoked Spanish paprika. I think the mushroom powder adds something special, but it can be hard to find. If you have it, use it, but I wouldn't make a special trip for it. I do love my paprika and the smoked variety adds depth. I think it's worth the bother to seek it out.

*I knew I wanted a meatless version of Chili con Carne, but I also knew I wanted something I could serve to my Texan friends who love their chili. Why would I bother worrying about what hardcore Chili con Carne aficionados think about my vegetarian chili? I had something to prove. A lot of vegetarian chili recipes taste great. But, for me, chili needs to be all about the chiles. Texans say that beans don't belong in chili, and I understand their doubts. After much experimenting, however, I realized the real issue was tomatoes! Tomatoes add a pleasant sweetness and some body, but they take the focus off the chile powder. My tomato-less Chili sin Carne is a recipe I would proudly serve to a Texan. It may be meatless but it's* muy macho—*and I don't mean just the heat, which is only moderate when using our chile powder.*   —Steve

*Most charro beans use bacon to give them a smoky flavor. Well, you can get that same delicious taste from chipotle chiles in adobo sauce. These small cans are versatile—some people add them to mayonnaise for a smoky, spicy topping.   —Steve*

# VEGETARIAN CHARRO BEANS

*2 cups cooked Rancho Gordo beans in their broth (such as Pinto, Rio Zape, or Eye of the Goat), cooked as directed on page 22*

*6 ounces dark beer*

*2 tablespoons extra-virgin olive oil*

*½ of an onion, chopped*

*2 cloves garlic, minced*

*2 chipotle chiles in adobo sauce, minced*

*½ pound mushrooms, sliced*

*Lime wedges for serving*

In a medium saucepan, warm the beans over medium-low heat; stir in the beer. The beans should be somewhat soupy. Add more beer if the liquid is too thick; increase heat and reduce the liquid if it's too thin.

In a large skillet, warm the oil over medium-low heat. Add the onion, garlic, and chiles; cook until soft, about 10 minutes. Add the mushrooms; cook until soft, about 10 minutes more.

Add mushroom mix to the pot of beans. Mix thoroughly and cook for another 10 minutes. Season to taste.

Serve with lime wedges.

*Serves 4 as a side dish*

*My friend Arnab Chakladar writes a biting and funny blog called* My Annoying Opinions, *and shared this recipe for our newsletter. He writes this about pressure cooking: "In my ancient Indian pressure cooker, I cook unsoaked beans over medium-low heat for about 25 minutes after the first whistle. I'm told Instant Pots don't whistle or seem like they're going to explode—I don't know how you can trust them."*   —Steve

# VAQUERO BEAN CURRY WITH POTATOES

*1 pound Rancho Gordo Vaquero beans, picked over and rinsed*

*1 stick Rancho Gordo Canela*

*½ teaspoon dried turmeric*

*2–3 dried red chiles*

*¾ tablespoon cumin seeds*

*¾ tablespoon coriander seeds*

*2 tablespoons peanut oil*

*1 large red onion, chopped*

*¾ tablespoon peeled and grated fresh ginger*

*¾ tablespoon grated or finely minced garlic*

*One 14.5-ounce can tomatoes or 2 cups chopped fresh tomatoes*

*Salt*

*Sugar*

*½ pound small round potatoes*

*Fresh cilantro for garnish*

*Flatbread, or warm cooked Basmatic rice for serving*

Cook the beans as directed on page 22, with the canela and turmeric. If using a pressure cooker (page 25), add the beans, canela, turmeric, and 4 cups of water. Cover and cook under pressure until beans are just tender. (The timing will vary, depending on the pressure cooker, but it should be about 25 minutes.)

In a skillet over medium heat, toast the chiles, cumin, and coriander until fragrant. Grind in a spice grinder or mortar.

Meanwhile, in a saucepan, warm oil over medium-low heat. Add the onion; cook until soft, about 10 minutes. Add ginger and garlic; cook for another minute or two until aromatic. Raise heat to medium; add the ground spices, mix thoroughly, and cook for another minute or two. Add the tomatoes, salt, and a pinch of sugar; cook, stirring occasionally, until the oil begins to separate, about 20 minutes.

Add the potatoes; stir to coat with the tomato mixture.

When the beans are cooked, add the beans and their liquid to the saucepan. Mix thoroughly, adding enough water to cover beans and potatoes by about 2 inches. Simmer, stirring occasionally, until the potatoes are tender, about 15 minutes. The sauce should be thickened but easily pourable; adjust with more water or broth as needed.

Garnish with cilantro and serve with flatbread, or over rice.

*Serves 6–8*

*Roasted sweet potatoes are a staple for quick dinners in our house. What better way to round out the meal than with beans and rice? The green sauce adds color and a bright herbaceous flavor. Store any extra sauce in the refrigerator and use it as a salad dressing or as a dipping sauce.* —Julia

# BLACK BEANS AND RICE WITH SWEET POTATO AND GREEN SAUCE

*2 cups cooked Rancho Gordo Midnight Black beans, cooked as directed on page 22*

*3 large sweet potatoes, peeled and sliced into rounds or wedges*

*4 tablespoons extra-virgin olive oil (divided use)*

*Rancho Gordo Stardust Dipping Powder or 100% Pure Chile Powder*

*Salt and pepper*

*For the Green Sauce:*

*1½ cups plain yogurt (or sour cream)*

*1 small bunch fresh cilantro, stems removed*

*2 green onions, chopped*

*1 garlic clove, chopped*

*1 small jalapeño chile, seeded and chopped (optional)*

*Juice of 1–2 limes*

*Salt*

*2 cups warm cooked white or brown rice*

In a small saucepan, warm the beans over low heat.

Preheat the oven to 400°F. Line a large baking sheet with foil and coat with 1 tablespoon of the olive oil. In a bowl, toss the sweet potatoes with the remaining 3 tablespoons olive oil and a liberal amount of Stardust, salt, and pepper. Spread the sweet potatoes on the baking sheet in a single layer; bake until soft, about 30 minutes. Raise the oven temperature to 450°F and bake until the edges of the sweet potatoes are caramelized, about 10 more minutes. Check the sweet potatoes often and move them around on the sheet to make sure they don't stick or burn.

To make the Green Sauce, place the yogurt, cilantro, green onion, garlic, and chile (if using) in a blender; blend until smooth. Add lime juice and salt to taste.

In a bowl, gently combine the rice and beans. Divide the rice-and-bean mixture among plates, top with sweet potatoes, and drizzle with the green sauce. Serve extra sauce at the table.

*Serves 4*

# COCONUT BROWN RICE AND BEANS

1 cup cooked Rancho Gordo Domingo Rojo beans in their broth, cooked as directed on page 22

¾ cup cold water

¾ cup unsweetened coconut milk

1-inch piece of Rancho Gordo Canela (true cinnamon)

3 whole cloves

1 cup brown rice, preferably Massa Organics

1 teaspoon sea salt

1 teaspoon grated fresh ginger

Cilantro or watercress for garnish (optional)

In a small saucepan, warm the beans over low heat.

In another small saucepan, add the water, coconut milk, canela, and cloves. Bring to a boil and then turn off heat; steep for 20 minutes. Strain, reserving the liquid and discarding the solids.

In a medium saucepan, add the rice, coconut milk mixture, salt, and ginger; bring to a boil over medium-high heat. Cook for 10 minutes, stirring occasionally. Reduce heat to very low and cover. Cook for 45 minutes, undisturbed, until the rice absorbs the liquid. Turn off heat; rest for 10 minutes.

Fluff the cooked rice with a fork; gently add the warm beans and cilantro or watercress, if using.

Serves 4 as a side dish

---

**BROWN RICE** I was an ardent hater of brown rice until I tried Massa Organics rice. It's nutty and rich and now I even prefer it over the white stuff for my everyday rice.

*Isn't it amazing how many cultures have rice and beans as a favorite dish? All over the world, you see this great combination. The best versions are a little soupy so that each grain of rice is covered with a thick, luscious sauce. Inspired by the Jamaican version of beans and rice, I was longing to see if coconut milk worked with brown rice and red beans as well as it does with the more traditional white rice. Friends, it's even better!* —Steve

This technique for cooking mushrooms was inspired by an entry on the blog He Cooks, She Cooks. *It's not intuitive, and yet it's the most sublime way to cook button mushrooms. I call it "carnitas" because the mushrooms cook in liquid and then fry in residual fat after the liquid evaporates, just like the classic Mexican pork dish. The flavor is intense! I've been using olive oil instead of the original recipe's butter, and I add a bay leaf or a sprig of fresh epazote during the cooking. If you want to make this a more substantial meal, serve over cooked brown rice.* —Steve

# HEIRLOOM BEAN AND MUSHROOM "CARNITAS" CASSEROLE

2 cups cooked Rancho Gordo Eye of the Goat beans (or other brown beans), cooked as directed on page 22, then drained

6 ounces canned whole peeled tomatoes (see note); plus ½ cup juice from the canned tomatoes

1 cup Mushroom Carnitas (see below)

2 garlic cloves, minced

1½ teaspoons fresh thyme

Salt to taste

5 very small fresh mozzarella balls (bocconccini)

For the Mushroom Carnitas:

2 cups sliced button mushrooms

2 garlic cloves, peeled

2 tablespoons extra-virgin olive oil

1 bay leaf (optional)

1 teaspoon sea salt

1 teaspoon dried Mexican oregano, preferably Rancho Gordo Oregano Indio

Preheat the oven to 375°F. Drain and roughly chop the tomatoes.

In a small casserole, combine all ingredients except the mozzarella. Stir well. Taste and adjust salt; the beans and mushrooms are likely to already be well-salted. Arrange the mozzarella balls on the top of the casserole and push them down into the liquid.

Bake, uncovered, for about 45 minutes, but start checking after 30 minutes. The liquid should be bubbling and the cheese starting to melt.

FOR THE MUSHROOM CARNITAS:

Place all the ingredients in a large saucepan; add enough water to not quite cover the mushrooms. Bring the liquid to a hard boil over high heat. Reduce heat to a gentle simmer; cook until the liquid has mostly evaporated, about 15 minutes, stirring to avoid scorching. Watch carefully: Once evaporation starts, things happen quickly. The mushrooms will start to sauté in the residual oil. Keep stirring until the mushrooms are golden brown. Remove from heat and use as a taco filling or in a casserole.

*Serves 4–6*

**TOMATOES** Some of you are thinking: "Why not just buy crushed tomatoes in a can if you're going to chop them up anyway?" I think the quality of those processed tomatoes is even worse than the whole ones. I suspect there's less tomato inside and you're paying for juice. Yes, I can be a pain. But I'm just trying to help.

# QUICK IDEAS No Recipe Needed

**REBOSERO BEANS** with steamed cauliflower and red salsa fresca

**CHRISTMAS LIMA BEANS** with marinated artichokes and fresh parsley

# QUICK IDEAS No Recipe Needed

**EYE OF THE GOAT BEANS** and wild rice topped with chopped pecans and pecan oil

**HEIRLOOM BEAN BROTH,** vegetable broth, boiled cactus paddles, and a poached egg

*Chapter 4*
# NON-NATIVES & GRAINS

Most of our crops are indigenous to the Americas, but Garbanzo beans are not. The state of commercial Garbanzo beans depressed me, so I asked our growers to add them to our mix. Garbanzo beans work in so many different cuisines, and I think hummus is one of the great dishes of all time. We've recently added black eyed peas to our lineup, another non-native—but often requested—bean.

Wild rice, posole, and quinoa are New World grains; they're also key components of a vegetarian pantry.

*This recipe calls for half a pound of Garbanzo beans. I would go ahead and cook a whole pound and use the other half for salads, soups ... or even another batch of hummus. I personally like my hummus simple, but there are lots and lots of variations. When I mentioned hummus on our Facebook page, many folks suggested adding a pinch of cumin.* —Steve

# A SIMPLE HUMMUS

*½ pound Rancho Gordo Garbanzo beans, picked over and rinsed (see page 22)*

*¼ of an onion, sliced*

*1 bay leaf*

*6 tablespoons tahini*

*2 tablespoons extra-virgin olive oil, plus more for drizzling*

*Juice of 1 lemon*

*3 garlic cloves, minced*

*Salt*

*Smoked Spanish paprika (optional)*

In a large saucepan, combine the Garbanzo beans and onion. Add enough water to cover beans by about 2 inches. Bring the liquid to a hard boil over high heat; cook for 10–15 minutes. Reduce heat to a gentle simmer; add the bay leaf, and cook until tender. Check the water level, adding more hot water to keep beans submerged.

Strain the beans, reserving ¼ cup for serving. Add the rest of the beans to the bowl of a food processor with the tahini, olive oil, lemon, garlic, and a pinch of salt; pulse until smooth. Taste and adjust the salt, tahini, and lemon. (You can also puree the hummus in a bowl using an immersion blender.)

Pour the hummus into a shallow bowl and draw a little pattern on the top. Gently drizzle your best olive oil over the hummus, letting it flow as it may. Dust with Spanish paprika and dot with the reserved garbanzo beans. Serve with crudites or pita.

*Serves 6–8*

# FRIED GARBANZO BEAN SNACK

1 teaspoon garlic powder

1 teaspoon Mexican oregano, preferably Rancho Gordo Oregano Indio

1 teaspoon Rancho Gordo Stardust Dipping Powder (optional)

Salt and freshly ground pepper

2 tablespoons extra-virgin olive oil

2 cups cooked Rancho Gordo Garbanzo beans, cooked as directed on page 22, then drained and patted dry

In a small bowl, combine the garlic powder, oregano, Stardust (if using), salt, and pepper; set aside.

In a small skillet, warm the olive oil over medium-high heat. Add the beans and spices; cook the mixture, shaking the pan occasionally, until most of the moisture is gone, about 7 minutes. The beans won't be crispy, but will look more like very small potatoes.

Drain the beans on a paper towel; taste and adjust the seasonings. Serve at room temperature.

*Serves 6–8*

**STARDUST DIPPING POWDER** is an addictive chile-lime mix for dusting fresh fruit, popcorn, beans, and even the rims of cocktail glasses. There is a running competition among the Rancho Gordo staff for the most creative way to use our Stardust powder! If you don't have any on hand for this recipe, you can substitute chile powder, and finish the dish off with a squeeze of lime.

*To serve during cocktail hour, or just for fun, we've adapted a classic Italian snack. I think this is a smart way to start a meal.* —Steve

*This classic soup from Mexico City has many versions but the constants seem to be Garbanzo beans, chipotle chiles, and chicken. For this version, I ditched the chicken and replaced it with more vegetables. You'll need to really focus on making a good broth, but that's a fun challenge.* —Steve

# VEGETARIAN CALDO TLALPEÑO

½ of a white onion, minced

2 chipotle chiles in adobo sauce, roughly chopped, with seeds and sauce

1 cup chopped tomatoes

2 garlic cloves, minced

1 tablespoon extra-virgin olive oil

6 cups vegetable broth (preferably homemade)

1 cup Rancho Gordo Garbanzo beans, cooked as directed on page 22, then drained

1 cup peeled, sliced carrots

2 small zucchini, sliced

Avocado cubes for garnish

Lime wedges for serving

In a blender, combine the onion, chiles, tomatoes, and garlic; puree until smooth.

In a stockpot or large saucepan, warm the oil over medium heat. Add the pureed vegetables; cook, stirring occasionally, until soft, about 10 minutes. Add the broth and bring to a simmer; cook, uncovered, for about 15 minutes.

Add the beans, carrots, and zucchini; continue to simmer until the carrots and zucchini are just tender and the beans are warm, about 10 minutes.

Ladle soup into warmed individual bowls, garnish with avocado, and serve immediately. Pass the lime wedges at the table.

*Serves 4–6*

*When our Meyer lemon trees are loaded with fruit, I make a batch of preserved lemons, then I use them with reckless abandon—in salad dressings, soups, marinades, and more. They are not a necessity here, but they really do add an extra punch that's hard to achieve with lemon zest and juice.* —Julia

# GARBANZO BEAN SALAD WITH CUCUMBER, TOMATO, AND ARUGULA

*2 tablespoons chopped preserved lemons or 1 tablespoon lemon zest*

*Juice of 1 lemon*

*3 tablespoons extra-virgin olive oil*

*Salt and freshly ground pepper*

*2 cups cooked Rancho Gordo Garbanzo beans, cooked as directed on page 22, then drained*

*¼ cup finely chopped red onion*

*1 English cucumber, chopped*

*1 cup halved cherry tomatoes*

*2 cups baby arugula*

*½ cup torn fresh mint*

*1 cup cooked Israeli couscous or quinoa*

In the bottom of a serving bowl, whisk together the preserved lemons (or zest), lemon juice, olive oil, salt, and pepper to taste. Add the beans, onion, cucumber, tomatoes, arugula, mint and couscous. Stir well to combine. Taste and adjust the seasonings.

*Serves 4–6*

*This is the perfect salad to bring to a picnic or as workday lunch. A picnic sounds nicer, of course. I beg you: Don't pour your bean-cooking broth down the drain. It's so, so delicous. I usually cook Garbanzo beans in my slow cooker and as soon as they are done (after about 4 hours on high), I excitedly ladle some of the cooking broth into a bowl and drink it. I guess that makes me a certified bean freak.* —Julia

# GARBANZO BEAN AND CABBAGE SLAW

¼ cup roasted, salted peanuts, plus extra for garnish

1 cup fresh cilantro leaves

Juice of 2 limes

1 tablespoon Rancho Gordo Pineapple Vinegar or rice wine vinegar

¼ cup extra-virgin olive oil

2 cups cooked Rancho Gordo Garbanzo beans, cooked as directed on page 22, then drained

2 cups shredded green cabbage

1 cup peeled, shredded carrots

3 green onions, sliced

Salt to taste

Use a blender or food processor to pulse the peanuts into crumbs. Add half the cilantro, the lime juice, and the vinegar; puree until smooth. Add the olive oil and puree again.

In a serving bowl, combine the beans, cabbage, carrots, green onions, and remaining cilantro. Toss with the dressing, season with salt, and garnish with chopped peanuts and more cilantro, if desired.

*Serves 2–4*

**VEGETABLE PREP** Buying preshredded cabbage or sliced cheese is ridiculous, I know. I try my best to avoid these things at the grocery store. I have found that prepping a few vegetables—slicing carrots, shredding cabbage, or roasting cauliflower—as soon as I get home from the store makes my life so much easier when I'm trying to whip up dinner on a busy weeknight.

# WILD RICE SALAD WITH XOCONOSTLE

8 tablespoons extra-virgin olive oil (divided use)

1 yellow onion, finely chopped (divided use)

1 small carrot, peeled and minced

½ celery stalk, minced

1 teaspoon salt

1 garlic clove, minced

1 cup Rancho Gordo California Wild Rice

2 ounces chopped Xoxoc Xoconostle Dulce (sweet dried prickly pears), or dried cran-berries

4 radishes, chopped

1 garlic clove, minced

1 teaspoon dried Mexican oregano, preferably Rancho Gordo Oregano Indio

Chopped flat-leaf parsley

2 tablespoons Rancho Gordo Banana Vinegar or white wine vinegar

Salt

2 ounces toasted pumpkin seeds

In a large saucepan, warm 2 tablespoons of the olive oil over medium heat. Add half of the onion, plus the carrot, celery, salt, and garlic; cook until soft, about 10 minutes. Add the wild rice; stir well. Add 2 cups water, raise heat to high, and bring to a boil for 5 minutes. Reduce heat to low; cover and cook for 50 minutes. The liquid should be absorbed and the rice should be tender. Cool to room temperature.

In a large bowl, combine the cooked wild rice, xoconostle, radishes, remaining onion, garlic, oregano, and parsley.

In a small bowl, whisk the vinegar, remaining oil, and salt; toss with the salad ingredients and top with pumpkin seeds.

Serves 6–8

**DRIED XOCONOSTLE** You can try another dried fruit but xoconostle are worth the bother of tracking down. We sell a few different types of dried xoconostle at Rancho Gordo, both sweet and salty.

*Like white rice, farro, and wheat berries, wild rice makes for a great salad. It's savory and substantial. I'd had wild rice salads with candied nuts or fruit and I experimented to see if it would work with xoconostle, the dried prickly pears made by my friends Yunuen and Gabriel of Xoxoc in Mexico. I've ended up making this salad a lot, especially since I have most of the ingredients on hand for a quick toss.*  —Steve

This dish is nothing like an Alfredo sauce with its heavy cream and cheese, but it satisfies in the same indulgent manner. I was expecting this to be "nice" and a good way to use up the last of a batch of Garbanzo beans. I was wrong: It was great. When we ate this, my son Nico and I looked at each other and smiled. This dish from Tuscany is a keeper.  —Steve

# PASTA WITH GARBANZO BEAN PUREE

¼ cup extra-virgin olive oil

1 large fresh rosemary sprig

2 garlic cloves, peeled

1½ cups cooked Rancho Gordo Garbanzo beans, cooked as directed on page 22, plus some of their broth

½ pound dried linguine

⅓ cup of grated pecorino cheese

Large handful of flat-leaf parsley, roughly chopped

In a skillet, warm the olive oil over low heat. Add the rosemary and garlic; sauté over very low heat for about 20 minutes. (The oil will infuse and the smell will be insane!) Remove the rosemary from the oil, and add the beans.

Blend the mixture with an immersion blender until smooth (or let cool slightly and process in batches in a blender or food processor), adding enough bean broth to make a thin sauce. If you add too much liquid, raise the heat and reduce the sauce.

Cook the pasta just short of al dente, then add it to the sauce to finish cooking. Add the cheese and parsley; toss gently and serve.

*Serves 4*

*After a gentle simmer, dried hominy opens up like a delicious flower and is ready to use in soups, stews and the classic southwestern and Mexican dish, Pozole (or Posole). Most of us think of it as an ingredient exclusively for Mexican cuisine, which is understandable, but it's a shame. Hominy is a delicious grain that knows no borders.* —Steve

# VEGETABLE SOUP WITH POSOLE

*1 cup dried Rancho Gordo White Corn Posole/Prepared Hominy (or 3 cups cooked posole)*

*3 thick slices white or yellow onion, plus 1 medium white onion, finely chopped*

*1 tablespoon olive oil*

*2 cloves garlic, minced*

*2 carrots, peeled and chopped into large chunks*

*1 celery stalk, chopped*

*1 teaspoon Mexican oregano, preferably Rancho Gordo Oregano Indio*

*1 small head broccoli, cut into small florets*

*6–8 cups vegetable broth or posole cooking liquid*

*Salt and pepper*

*Lime wedges for serving*

If you are starting with dried posole, soak it for 6–8 hours. Strain the posole and discard the soaking liquid. In a large pot, add the soaked posole, about 3 quarts of water, and the onion slices. Bring to a hard boil for 10 minutes, then reduce heat to a gentle simmer and cook until soft, 2–3 hours. The posole will flower, like popcorn, when it's finished. Strain the posole, reserving both the corn and cooking broth.

Heat the oil in a large pot over medium heat. Add the chopped onion, garlic, carrots, and celery, and cook until soft, about 5 minutes. Add oregano and broccoli; stir until all ingredients are well mixed. Add 6 cups of posole cooking broth and/or vegetable broth. Bring to a boil, then reduce heat and simmer until the vegetables are soft, about 20 minutes. Stir in the cooked posole and continue to simmer until the posole is warmed through.

Add salt and pepper to taste. Serve in individual bowls and pass lime wedges at the table.

*Serves 8*

*I am a big fan of falafel, but the thought of making it from scratch is overwhelming. So here is a lazy version—a dinner you can throw together in less than 20 minutes if you have the ingredients on hand. Tzatziki is an extremely versatile sauce and you can find many quality versions at the grocery store if you don't have time to make it yourself. Steve likes to put a dollop of it on a bowl of beans, of course.*  —Julia

# FRIED GARBANZO BEAN PITAS

For the Tzatziki:

*1 cup plain Greek yogurt*

*½ of a cucumber, chopped or shredded, and drained*

*Juice of 1 lemon*

*1 garlic clove, minced*

*2 tablespoon minced fresh dill and/or mint*

*Salt*

*2 cups Fried Garbanzo Beans (page 126)*

*4 pita breads, halved and warmed in the oven*

*Chopped tomatoes, chopped cucumbers, chopped red onion, and/or lettuce for serving*

FOR THE TZATZIKI:

Combine the yogurt, cucumber, lemon, garlic, mint, and dill in a bowl. Add salt to taste.

TO SERVE:

Set out the Fried Garbanzo Beans, Tzatziki, warmed pita, and any other toppings you'd like and let diners create their own pitas.

*Serves 4*

**FRESH MINT AND DILL** are not always easy to find, unless you have some growing in your garden. If you don't want to bother seeking out both, you can use 2 tablespoons of one or the other for the Tzatziki, or even fresh parsley if that's what you have on hand.

# QUICK IDEAS No Recipe Needed

**BLACK EYED PEAS** with broth and wilted stinging nettles

# QUICK IDEAS No Recipe Needed

**GARBANZO BEANS** with sauteed chard and carrots, topped with puff pastry

**GARBANZO BEANS** with broth, potato, onion, saffron, and fresh parsley

# COMPOST BROTH

One of my favorite recent cookbooks has been *Decolonize Your Diet*. Luz Calvo and Catriona Rueda Esquibel offer a cuisine based on pre-Conquest foods, mostly vegan and vegetarian. Why not think about how great the Mexican diet was in 1491? The foundation was beans, chiles, and corn. Occasionally there was deer, rabbit, or fish. Delicious greens were foraged.

In the book, they have a corncob broth. It's naturally sweet and delicious. It got me thinking about other things to add to a vegetable broth. Why not onion tops, carrot tops, or garlic skins? All the things that normally get thrown into the compost might be better served as broth ingredients. I started saving everything in a bag in my fridge and for the last few Sundays, I've been making this "compost" broth and using it throughout the week when I needed a flavorful liquid.

To make the broth, I put about 2 cups of vegetable scraps, plus a bay leaf and a handful of peppercorns, in a pot and cover with 6–8 cups of water. I simmer it for 2–3 hours, then let the broth cool a bit in the pot. Then I strain out the solids.

I've also made what I call garbage soup. I use the compost broth along with any beans I have left over. The recipe is simple: Onion and garlic sautéed in olive oil, with pureed tomatoes and our Oregano Indio. Then beans. Then the broth. Then a handful of chopped lambsquarters.

I've been growing lambsquarters— *Chenopodium album*, also known as goosefoot in the South or *quelites* in Spanish—in our parking lot at Rancho Gordo. A handful chopped up and added to this mess is perfect.   —*Steve*

# BEAN BROTH

This may seem painfully obvious but extra bean broth is like gold. Here at Rancho Gordo the retail staff makes beans for sampling in a slow cooker and they do an incredible job of it. Most afternoons you'll find me sneaking a shot of bean broth as a late-in-the-day pick-me-up. I've even started taking the extra broth home and I use it to poach eggs, thin out sauces and of course a base for soup.   —*Steve*

# WILD RICE BROTH

I've written a lot about using bean broth, on its own or in combination with another broth, as the base for your soup.

I had a moment of inspiration while making wild rice recently. I sautéed some onion, garlic, celery, and carrot in a little olive oil. Then I added a pound of Rancho Gordo Wild Rice. I covered it with water by about 3 inches, brought it to a full boil for 10 minutes, then reduced it to a simmer, covered, until the rice was cooked, about 50 minutes. There was a lot of extra liquid, so I strained the rice and used the liquid as broth. Friends, it was incredible: Dense, earthy and delicious. The rice was perfect, too.

Using the wild rice broth as a soup base, I made a bunch of different soups. My favorite used half wild rice broth and half Alubia Blanca bean broth. I added some beans and some sautéed mushrooms. Mushrooms and wild rice like each other a lot, and the creamy beans made the whole thing a party.   —*Steve*

# ROASTED VEGETABLE BROTH

I'm a roasting fanatic. It requires very little active cooking time and the flavor payoff is huge. I roast vegetables every weekend and use them in various dishes during the week. You can usually find me on a Sunday night hovered over a baking sheet, snacking on little golden bits of roasted vegetables.

I recently made a roasted vegetable broth and was blown away by the depth of flavor it added to my soup. You can use pretty much any vegetables you have on hand, but make sure to include at least two aromatics (garlic, onion, leeks, shallot, etc.).

I preheated the oven to 400°F. While the oven was preheating, I peeled and quarted 1 onion, chopped 2 carrots, halved and rinsed 1 large leek and 1 fennel bulb, and halved 2 large tomatoes. I put all this in a roasting pan and threw in a few unpeeled garlic cloves and a celery stalk. I tossed everything with olive oil and some salt, then roasted it for about 45 minutes, stirring occasionally. Then, I scraped the roasted vegetables into a pot and added 8 cups of water. (If I had had the time, I would have deglazed the roasting pan with white wine to get all the caramelized bits off the bottom.) I added a bay leaf and some fresh thyme to the pot and simmered it for about an hour. Then I strained the solids and let the broth cool before storing.    —*Julia*

# ROASTED POBLANO CHILE RAJAS

One of my favorite ways to eat beans is with roasted poblano chiles. I think green bell peppers are okay but you really can't compare them to big, meaty poblanos. Poblanos are juicy and versatile, and they go well with beans, making them my ideal pepper.

Here in California, a lot of stores mismark fresh poblano chiles as pasilla peppers. Most of Mexico knows this chile as a poblano.

This chile is almost never eaten without roasting and removing the skin first. I've done it a million times and I think I can do it in my sleep. But I do know it's an odd technique, so I'll fill you in on how I do it.

If you have just one or two peppers, it's very easy to roast them right beneath the fire of a gas oven. If you have a lot, or you're working with an electric range, you can roast them on a comal or a well-heated cast iron skillet. At first, I discounted this method but, really, it's nice not to have to keep a close watch to prevent overcharring. You have to rotate the chiles and turn them as they char, but you don't have to hover as much as you would with an open flame.

This method can leave a lot of unblistered skin, so I use my BernzOmatic torch to obsessively fill in all the green gaps with

its unforgiving heat. When the entire chile is charred, you're done. (If you don't own a torch, you can be a little less obsessive; it will taste almost as delicious.)

A lot of instructions have you place roasted chiles in a plastic bag and let them sweat. I find the idea of sweating in plastic unpleasant, and I'm betting the chiles do, too. I opt for a mixing bowl with a plate on top, if I have just a few chiles, or a big old paper grocery bag for larger batches. Let them rest about 15 minutes, covered and undisturbed.

I've seen Diana Kennedy pull the whole skin off a roasted chile with one stroke using just her fingers. After years of practice, I can almost do this, but not quite. I end up using my trusty kitchen knife to separate and remove the skin.

You also want to remove the seeds inside. If you're making Chiles Rellenos (page 93), find a weak section on the chile's side, make a slit with your knife, and remove the seeds from there. For *rajas*, we want just the chile "meat," so chop off the top and remove the seed head along with all the seeds. You can scrape with the dull end of your knife to remove any stray seeds.

I've seen recipes suggest you rinse peeled and seeded chiles in cold water. I'm sure there are situations where you want a super-clean chile, but I can't believe you're not sending flavor down the drain. A few char marks or seeds aren't going to harm things, and they may even help. You also will find some lovely juices collect as the chiles cool down. Save them!

Now you can take the chiles and fry them with oil, onion, garlic, and oregano, and you have beautiful *rajas* to enjoy. Classically, they're a great match for eggs, or paired with cheese as a stuffing for tamales. I've fried them with olive oil, garlic, and onion, then pureed them as a sauce for pasta. Your options are unlimited.

# ROMESCO SAUCE

2 slices of crusty bread, crusts removed, cubed

½ cup almonds

4 garlic cloves, peeled

2 medium tomatoes

2 red bell peppers

¼–½ cup olive oil

2 tablespoons red wine vinegar or sherry vinegar

1 tablespoon smoked Spanish paprika

Salt


Preheat oven to 375°F.

Line a rimmed baking sheet with aluminum foil. Place the bread cubes, almonds, garlic, and tomatoes on the baking sheet; roast until the almonds are fragrant and the bread is just starting to brown, about 10 minutes. Remove the almonds and bread from the tray; set aside. Continue roasting the garlic and tomatoes until soft, about 20 minutes more. Remove the sheet from the oven, and let cool slightly. Skin the tomatoes and peel the garlic, then set them aside.

Raise the oven temperature to 500°F; roast the peppers until the skins have charred, about 30 minutes, turning until all sides are blistered.

Place the peppers in a bowl and cover with a plate; let sit until cool enough to handle, about 20 minutes. Remove the charred skin, seeds, and cores.

Place the bread, almonds, garlic, tomatoes, peppers, olive oil, vinegar, paprika, and salt in the bowl of a food processor. Process until a chunky sauce forms. Add salt to taste.

# CASCABEL CHILE SALSA

10 Rancho Gordo Cascabel Chiles, wiped clean, seeds and veins removed, seeds reserved

One 12-ounce can whole peeled tomatoes, drained

3 garlic cloves, roughly chopped

½ teaspoon salt

About ⅔ cup water

On a dry skillet or comal over medium heat, toast the chiles, turning them constantly until warmed, about 3 minutes. Remove from heat.

Toast the chile seeds to a deep golden brown, turning constantly or they will burn.

Process all the ingredients in a blender, adding a little more water if necessary; the sauce should have a loose consistency, but it will thicken as it stands.

# ITALIAN-SYLE SALSA VERDE

1½ cups mixed fresh herbs, such as flat-leaf parsley, oregano, rosemary, thyme, and sage

¼ cup brined capers, drained

½ cup extra-virgin olive oil

Zest and juice of 1 lemon

Sea salt and freshly ground pepper

On a cutting board, mince all of the herbs together. Add the capers and mince again. Transfer to a bowl and whisk in the olive oil, lemon zest, and juice. Season with salt and pepper. (You can also prepare in a food processor.)

# MEXICAN-STYLE SALSA VERDE

5–6 medium tomatillos, peeled and rinsed

1 large slice white onion, chopped fine

4 serrano chiles, minced

3 garlic cloves, minced

Salt

1 teaspoon dried Mexican oregano, preferably Rancho Gordo Mexican Oregano or Rancho Gordo Oregano Indio

Juice of ½ lime

Small handful of cilantro, chopped fine


On a dry skillet or comal, roast the tomatillos over high heat. Rotate them often so they get nicely charred but don't turn into charcoal. They should be soft in about 5–8 minutes.

Meanwhile, in your *molcajete* or mortar, mash the onion, chiles, garlic, and salt until they become a nice goo. (The finer your chop, the less work this will be.)

When the tomatillos are soft and hissing, remove from heat and allow them to cool. Chop fine and add to the *molcajete*. Mash again until well blended. Add the lime juice and cilantro.


# REQUESÓN

1 tablespoon extra virgin olive oil

About ¼ cup chopped fermented or pickled chiles and onions (or 1 fresh serrano chile, seeded and minced, plus ½ of a white onion), minced

1–2 garlic cloves, minced

2 cups good ricotta cheese

Handful of fresh epazote leaves, chopped

In a large pan, warm the olive oil over medium heat. Add the chile, onion, and garlic. Cook, stirring, until soft, about 3 minutes.

Add the ricotta and stir until well mixed. Cook until the ricotta begins to dry, about 3 minutes. Right before removing from heat, add the epazote; mix well.

# BIBLIOGRAPHY

*Cucina Povera* by Pamela Sheldon Johns (2011, Andrews McMeel Publishing)

*Decolonize Your Diet* by Luz Calvo and Catriona Rueda Esquibel (2015, Arsenal Pulp Press)

*Delicias Vegetarianas de Mexico* by Gloria Cardona (2001, Editorial Pax México)

*In My Kitchen* by Deborah Madison (2017, Ten Speed Press)

*Mexico Sano* by Pia Quintana Berstain (2012, AmbarDeseno)

*Moro* by Sam & Sam Clark (2003, Ebury Press); *Casa Moro* by Sam & Sam Clark (2004, Ebury Press); *Moro East* by Sam & Sam Clark (2007, Ebury Press)

*Mozza at Home* by Nancy Silverton (2016, Knopf)

*On Vegetables* by Jeremy Fox (2017, Phaidon)

*Potager* by Georgeanne Brennan (2000, Chronicle Books)

*The Everlasting Meal* by Tamar Adler (2011, Scribner)

*The New Vegetarian Cooking for Everyone* by Deborah Madison (2014, Ten Speed Press)

*Tradiciones de la Cocina Hñähñu del Valle del Mezquital* by Edith Yesenia Peña Sánchez and Lila Hernandez Albarran (2014, Conaculta)

*Vegetariano* by Patricia Quintana (2010, Editorial Oceano)

# INDEX